Cinnamon
MORNINGS

Also by Pamela Lanier

The Complete Guide to Bed and Breakfasts, Inns and
    Guesthouses in the United States and Canada

Elegant Small Hotels: A Connoisseur's Guide

All Suite Hotel Guide

Condo Vacations

Golf Resorts: The Complete Guide

Golf Resorts International

22 Days in Alaska

Cinnamon
MORNINGS

by
Pamela Lanier

RUNNING PRESS
PHILADELPHIA, PENNSYLVANIA

Library of Congress Cataloging-in-Publication Number 91–50908
ISBN: 1–56138–082–2

Judy Jacobs, Project Coordinator
Karen Young Joffe, Culinary Editor
Mariposa Valdes, Editor, Second Edition
Cover design by Toby Schmidt
Cover illustration by Jack Coleman
Interior illustration by Lisa Umlauf Roese
Interior design by Jacqueline Spadaro
Typography: CG Palacio with Signet Roundhand by
Commcor Communications Corporation, Philadelphia, PA
Printed in the United States

This book can be ordered by mail from the publisher.
Please include $2.50 for postage and handling for each copy.
But try your bookstore first!
Running Press
Book Publishers
125 South 22nd Street
Philadelphia, Pennsylvania 19103

This book is dedicated to our children and the hope that the earth they inherit will be as beautiful and bountiful as the one we enjoy.

Many thanks to the cooks who took time to send us their recipes and suggestions and to those inns who provided us with line drawings of their establishments.

Special thanks to all my friends who helped with this book, and especially Judy Jacobs, project coordinator, Karen Young Joffe, culinary editor, and Mariposa Valdes, second edition editor, whose excellent work is evident throughout.

Contents

49   *Part 2 — Brunch*

109 — *Part 3 — Teatime*

Part 4 – Hors d'Oeuvres 137

Index 154

Bed and breakfast inns (B&Bs) allow the traveller to be immersed in the elegance of an antebellum plantation, to sleep in an historic landmark, to get away from it all on a Colorado ranch or to try houseboating in San Francisco. Whatever the setting, the personal and convivial atmosphere of a B & B provides the chance to make new friends and relax while vacationing. All the little B & B extras that one doesn't expect from an impersonal hotel add up to a special travel experience that is winning over all who travel the B & B route.

Of course, breakfast is an essential ingredient in the B & B experience. This cookbook is a collection of innkeepers' favorite recipes of outstanding regional American cuisine, from Southern biscuits and pecan pie to Northeastern blueberry muffins to Southwestern huevos rancheros. And because brunch, teatime and the cocktail hour are also common culinary customs in America's inns, we include B & B dishes to be served at these times as well. Some will spark the imagination of even the most discriminating gourmet, while others will be perfect for that hectic Sunday morning when you want to do something special but haven't got much time or energy.

Most of the recipes are simple and easy to prepare, but they cover a wide range of cooking styles from a diverse variety of kitchens. Some chefs are precise and detailed in their instructions; others leave much up to the individual cook. To make the preparation of the dishes easier, we have endeavored to standardize the measurements and procedures— without detracting from the unique style of each contributing chef. In addition to the recipes, we have included a short profile of each inn, along with reservation information, to help you with your future travel plans. When you visit each inn, you can taste its specialties for yourself.

Where two recipes from the same inn follow one another, reservation information follows the second recipe. Our charge-card key is as follows: MC equals MasterCard, AE equals American Express, V equals Visa, DC is Diner's Club, CB is Carte Blanche.

A price code is shown to give you an idea of the inns' prices, which are subject to change. Generally, Inexpensive is under $40; Moderate is $40 to $80; Expensive is $80 to $125; Very Expensive is over $125.

Bon appetit and sweet dreams!

Introduction

Part 1

BREAKFAST

Breakfast

At the heart of every traveller's dreams is an inn where everything possible is done to please the guests. Thanks to abundant fresh produce and the creativity of their kitchens, America's innkeepers have created some of the most imaginative and delicious dishes ever to grace a breakfast table.

These recipes offer a glimpse of the diversity of America's regional cuisine. The style, of course, varies regionally as well as from inn to inn, but with the recipes on the following pages, you can create these treats over and over again.

The variety is not just in the food, however. There are just as many kinds of breakfasts as there are inns. Luxury establishments pride themselves on exquisite cuisine graciously presented. At the Red Clover Inn in Mendon, Vermont, the innkeeper—who is also the chef—delights his guests with candlelit breakfasts with classical music playing in the background. Country and small town inns often offer very substantial breakfasts with several choices of entrées, freshly baked fruit breads, juices and cereal. The call to breakfast at Captain Jefferd's Inn in Kennebunkport, Maine, is the theme music from *Upstairs/Downstairs*. Guests assemble around the edge of a banquet table flanked by a dozen hand-painted chairs, are personally introduced, and then are served by a white-jacketed waiter.

Other inns provide breakfast at small tables for individual parties, where the food is either served to your exact specifications or is the day's special dish. At Santa Fe's Grant Corner Inn, individual hearty breakfasts consist of separate sideboards: one for beverages, including several kinds of coffees and teas; another for cereals, granola and cornflakes; and the entrée. In addition, a plate of fresh fruit and a basket of sweet rolls and breads are served at your table.

Of course, food is not the only factor that contributes to an enjoyable eating experience. The mood of the meal is also created by the place setting, the china, the tablecloth, the vase of flowers in the center of the table and the smile on the host or hostess's face.

Pamela Lanier's Hungarian Coffee Cake

1 cup white sugar	1 cup buttermilk
1 cup brown sugar	2 eggs
1 cup shortening (butter or margarine)	1 teaspoon vanilla
	½ teaspoon salt
3 cups all-purpose flour	1 teaspoon baking powder
½ cup chopped nuts	1 teaspoon baking soda
1½ teaspoons cinnamon	

Preheat oven to 350°. Combine the first 6 ingredients. Take out 1 level cup and set aside for topping.

To the remaining mixture add the second column of ingredients.

Mix will be slightly lumpy. Pour into 2″×8″ cake or pie pans (2 or 3). Cover with the 1 cup of reserved nut mix and bake at 350° for 20 or 25 minutes. Do not over bake. Will stay fresh for 4 days. Serves 16.

I'm too busy visiting inns to run one, but like a lot of people, I've dreamed of becoming an innkeeper. If you share the dream, we have an information packet for prospective innkeepers you will like (and it's free!). Send a self addressed stamped envelope to:

Innkeeper Information
℅ The Complete Guide to Bed and Breakfasts,
    Inns and Guesthouses
P.O. Box 20467
Oakland, California 94620–0467

MOUNTAIN VIEW INN

Strings of Flats

Stacks of these griddle cakes were consumed in great quantity in the old lumbering camps, where they were known as flannel cakes (for the flannel shirts worn by lumberjacks) and as strings of flats (as in flatcars, the railroad cars that carried the lumber to market).

2 egg whites	2 tablespoons sugar
1 cup all-purpose flour	2 egg yolks
1 tablespoon baking powder	1 cup milk
½ teaspoon salt	2 tablespoons hot bacon grease

Beat egg whites until stiff. Sift together flour, baking powder, salt and sugar. Mix yolks and milk together and stir quickly into dry ingredients. Gently fold in beaten egg whites. After mixture is relatively smooth, fold in bacon grease. Cook pancakes on a hot grill. Serve with home-cured bacon, butter and lots of Vermont maple syrup. Serves 2 to 4, depending on appetites.

MOUNTAIN VIEW INN
Route 17, RFD Box 69
Waitsfield, Vermont
05673
(802) 496–2426

No credit cards
Moderate

The antique-filled Mountain View Inn has seven guestrooms. Homecooked country meals are served around a large harvest table.

Mountain View Inn
Waitsfield, Vermont

R I C H M O N D   I N N

Sausage and Egg Casserole

1 pound sausage
½ pound grated sharp cheese
½ teaspoon dry mustard
½ teaspoon paprika

1 teaspoon salt
1 cup sour cream
10 to 16 eggs (depending on
    crowd)

Preheat oven to 325°. Cook and drain sausage. Spray 2 or 3 quart dish with vegetable spray. Put half of the cheese on bottom of dish. Mix spices with sour cream and mix with sausage. Spread over grated cheese. (This much can be done the night before.) Beat eggs and pour over sausage mixture. Sprinkle remaining cheese on top. Bake at 325° for 25–30 minutes or until eggs are set. Serves 8 to 14.

W E S T   M O U N T A I N   I N N

Ooey Gooey

4 large slices of bread
4 tablespoons mayonnaise
8 eggs, fried

2 cups grated Vermont ched-
    dar cheese
1 teaspoon paprika

Spread slices of bread with mayonnaise. Top each slice with 2 fried eggs and grated Vermont cheddar cheese. Melt under a broiler. Lightly sprinkle paprika on melted cheese to enhance flavor and add color. Serves 4.

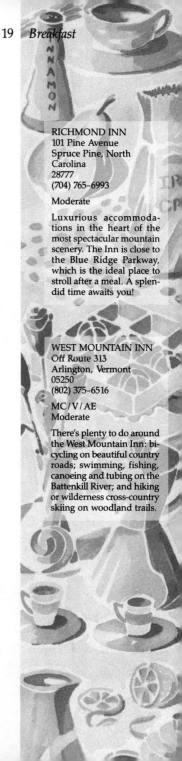

RICHMOND INN
101 Pine Avenue
Spruce Pine, North
Carolina
28777
(704) 765–6993

Moderate

Luxurious accommodations in the heart of the most spectacular mountain scenery. The Inn is close to the Blue Ridge Parkway, which is the ideal place to stroll after a meal. A splendid time awaits you!

WEST MOUNTAIN INN
Off Route 313
Arlington, Vermont
05250
(802) 375–6516

MC / V / AE
Moderate

There's plenty to do around the West Mountain Inn: bicycling on beautiful country roads; swimming, fishing, canoeing and tubing on the Battenkill River; and hiking or wilderness cross-country skiing on woodland trails.

MILLBROOK INN
RFD Box 62, Route 17
Waitsfield, Vermont
05673
(802) 496-2405

MC / V
Expensive

Guests can relax in this
charming six-room country
inn's unhurried atmosphere
and revel in its candlelit
dinners.

MILLBROOK, A COUNTRY INN

Pancakes à la Millbrook

2 cups all-purpose flour
1 teaspoon salt
2 tablespoons sugar
4 teaspoons baking powder
2 eggs, lightly beaten

2½ cups milk
2 tablespoons butter, melted
1 pint strawberries or raspberries (optional)

Mix flour, salt, sugar and baking powder in a large bowl. In another bowl, whisk eggs and milk together with a wire whisk. Stir in butter. Pour wet ingredients (eggs, milk and butter mixture) over dry ingredients (flour, salt, sugar and baking powder) and mix with a wooden spoon until just blended. The batter should be lumpy. Pour ¼ cup batter per pancake onto a hot griddle. (For blueberry or strawberry pancakes, sprinkle fresh blueberries or sliced fresh strawberries on the pancakes as soon as you pour the batter onto griddle.) Cook until cakes are full of air bubbles on top and lightly browned on underside. Flip over to brown the other side. Serves 6.

Millbrook, A Country Inn
Waitsfield, Vermont

TEN INVERNESS WAY

Banana Buttermilk Buckwheat Pancakes

1 cup all-purpose flour
½ cup whole wheat flour
½ cup buckwheat flour
2 tablespoons sugar
1 teaspoon salt
1 teaspoon baking soda

4 teaspoons baking powder
2 eggs, lightly beaten
4 tablespoons butter, melted
1½ cups buttermilk
½ cup milk
2 ripe bananas, mashed

In a large bowl, combine all-purpose flour, whole wheat flour, buckwheat flour, sugar, salt, baking soda and baking powder. In another bowl, combine remaining ingredients. Add liquid mixture to the dry ingredients, stirring well. Drop by ⅓ cupfuls onto a 350° griddle. Serves 4 to 6.

STONEHURST MANOR

Cornmeal and Bacon Pancakes

⅓ cup yellow cornmeal
1 cup all-purpose flour
1 teaspoon salt
2 teaspoons baking powder
1 egg

1¼ cup milk
1 tablespoon bacon fat,
    melted
2 strips bacon, cooked and
    crumbled

Mix together cornmeal, flour, salt and baking powder. In a separate bowl, beat the egg, add milk and then bacon fat. Stir this mixture slowly into the dry ingredients, mixing well. The batter should be fairly thin; add more milk if necessary. Finally mix in crumbled bacon. Cook pancakes in a skillet or on a griddle. Serve with butter and maple syrup. Serves 4.

TEN INVERNESS WAY
10 Inverness Way
Inverness, California
94937
(415) 669–1648

No credit cards
Moderate

This five-room inn is located an hour or so north of San Francisco and not far from the scenic beauty of Point Reyes National Seashore.

STONEHURST MANOR
P.O. Box 1937
Rt. 16
North Conway,
New Hampshire
03860
(603) 356–3271

MC / V / AE
Moderate to very expensive

The elegance of another era pervades this beautiful 24-room English-style country inn with rooms in every price range. The Stonehurst Manor is situated on 33 pine-forested acres.

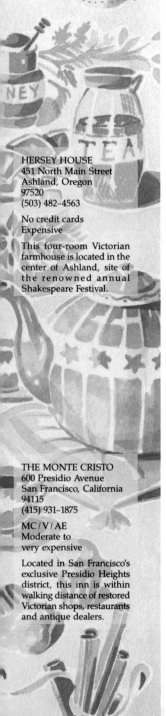

HERSEY HOUSE
451 North Main Street
Ashland, Oregon
97520
(503) 482–4563

No credit cards
Expensive

This four-room Victorian
farmhouse is located in the
center of Ashland, site of
the renowned annual
Shakespeare Festival.

THE MONTE CRISTO
600 Presidio Avenue
San Francisco, California
94115
(415) 931–1875

MC / V / AE
Moderate to
very expensive

Located in San Francisco's
exclusive Presidio Heights
district, this inn is within
walking distance of restored
Victorian shops, restaurants
and antique dealers.

H E R S E Y   H O U S E
Gingerbread Pancakes

This recipe comes from Dee Maaske, an actress who has performed with the Ashland Shakespeare Festival.

2 ½ cups all-purpose flour
5 teaspoons baking powder
1 ½ teaspoons salt
1 teaspoon baking soda
1 teaspoon cinnamon
½ teaspoon ginger

¼ cup molasses
2 cups milk
2 eggs, lightly beaten
6 tablespoons butter, melted
1 cup raisins

Sift together flour, baking powder, salt, soda and spices. Combine molasses and milk and add eggs, stirring to blend. Stir in melted butter. Add molasses mixture to dry ingredients. Stir only until moistened. Mix in raisins. Cook on a hot griddle, using ¼ cup batter for each pancake. Serves 8.

T H E   M O N T E   C R I S T O
Gooseberry Pancakes

1 cup whole wheat pastry
  flour
½ cup buckwheat flour
½ cup unbleached all-
  purpose flour
3 teaspoons baking powder
1 teaspoon salt

1 tablespoon brown sugar or
  honey
3 eggs, lightly beaten
2 cups milk
1 stick (4 ounces) butter,
  melted
1 cup gooseberries,
  cooked or canned

Sift flours with baking powder, salt and sugar (not honey). Beat together eggs, milk and melted butter. If using honey, add it to the milk and eggs mixture. Combine liquids with dry ingredients, stirring until just barely mixed. Fold in gooseberries. Cook on a hot griddle or in a greased frying pan. Serve with maple syrup and butter. Serves 6.

HARBOR HOUSE BY THE SEA

Souffléed Apple Pancakes

¼ cup (½ stick) unsalted butter

2 tart apples, peeled, cored and thickly sliced

¾ cups half-and-half

½ cup all-purpose flour

¼ teaspoon salt

3 egg yolks, lightly beaten

2 tablespoons unsalted butter, melted and cooled to room temperature

3 egg whites

pinch of cream of tartar

pinch of salt

1 tablespoon sugar

1 tablespoon butter

Preheat broiler.

In a stainless steel sauté pan or enameled skillet, melt the butter and sauté the apple slices, turning them carefully while cooking so they do not break. Cook until tender (about 6 minutes).

In a bowl, combine half-and-half, flour, ¼ teaspoon salt, egg yolks (one at a time) and the melted butter. In another bowl, beat the egg whites with cream of tartar and salt until they hold soft peaks. Add the sugar and continue beating until the whites hold stiff peaks. Stir ¼ of the whites into the batter to lighten it, then gently fold in the remaining whites. Melt 1 tablespoon butter in a flameproof 10″ skillet (with an 8″ bottom) over moderate heat. When it is hot, add half of the batter, spreading it evenly with a spatula. Cook the pancake for 3 minutes. Arrange half of the apple slices decoratively over the pancake, and put the pancake under the broiler, 4″ from the source of heat, for 2 to 3 minutes or until puffed and golden brown. Slide the pancake onto a serving plate and keep warm. Make another pancake in the same manner with the remaining batter and apple slices. Serve the pancakes with maple syrup. Serves 4 as a breakfast dish or 8 (cut pancakes into wedges) as a dessert.

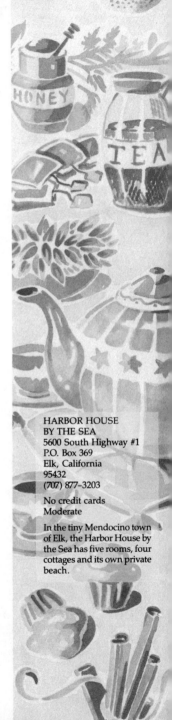

HARBOR HOUSE
BY THE SEA
5600 South Highway #1
P.O. Box 369
Elk, California
95432
(707) 877-3203

No credit cards
Moderate

In the tiny Mendocino town of Elk, the Harbor House by the Sea has five rooms, four cottages and its own private beach.

HUMPHREY HUGHES
HOUSE
29 Ocean Street
Cape May, New Jersey
08204
(609) 884-4428

MC / V / AE
Expensive

A restored Victorian home
in the historic seaside town
of Cape May, the Hum-
phrey Hughes House
serves a special Sunday
breakfast.

HILL FARM INN
R.R. 2, Box 2015
Arlington, Vermont
05250
(802) 375-2269

MC / V
Moderate

Hiking, fishing and full
country breakfasts are just a
few of the pleasures await-
ing guests at this seven-
room, three-cabin establishment, which has been in
operation for more than 75
years.

HUMPHREY HUGHES HOUSE
Golden Granola

1½ cups Quaker Old-Fashioned Oats	½ teaspoon cinnamon ⅛ cup butter, melted
½ cup chopped nuts, any kind	⅛ cup honey ½ teaspoon vanilla
½ cup shredded coconut	½ cup raisins or dried fruit

Preheat oven to 350°.

Mix oats, nuts, coconut and cinnamon in an ungreased baking dish. (To increase crispiness, one cup of cornflakes can
be substituted for 1 cup of oats.) Combine melted butter,
honey and vanilla. Pour over dry ingredients and mix. Bake
granola for 30 to 40 minutes, stirring every 5 to 10 minutes
to prevent burning. When evenly golden-colored, remove
and, while cooling, add raisins or fruit. Serves 12. Recipe can
be doubled and stored in tightly-covered containers.

HILL FARM INN
Hill Farm Inn French Toast

4 eggs	½ teaspoon vanilla
1 cup milk	8 slices homemade white
4 teaspoons sugar	bread, cut thickly
¼ teaspoon salt	

In a 13" by 9" baking dish, beat eggs, milk, sugar, salt and
vanilla until fluffy. Add bread to dish, turning after it has
soaked up about half of the mixture. When the bread is
thoroughly soaked, use a pancake turner to transfer it to a
hot buttered griddle (370°). Cook about 4 minutes on each
side, or until golden brown. Serve with Vermont maple syrup.
Serves 4 to 8.

T H E   S W A G

Swag Granola Cereal

1½ cups rolled oats
¼ cup sesame seeds
½ cup sunflower seeds
½ cup shredded unsweetened
　　coconut
½ cup wheat germ
¼ cup bran

½ cup almonds
¼ cup oil
¼ cup honey
½ teaspoon vanilla extract
½ teaspoon almond extract
raisins or other dried fruit,
　　as desired

Preheat oven to 300°.

Tumble together oats, sesame seeds, sunflower seeds, coconut, wheat germ, bran and almonds in a big bowl. Heat oil and honey together in saucepan until thin and fairly hot. Remove from heat and stir in vanilla and almond extracts. Pour over dry ingredients and stir to coat evenly. Spread in single layers on jelly roll pans and toast in oven, stirring from time to time, until evenly browned. Remove from oven and allow to cool thoroughly. Stir in raisins or other dried fruit. Serves 8 to 10. Recipe can be doubled and stored in tightly-covered containers.

The Swag
Waynesville, North Carolina

THE SWAG
Route 2, P.O. Box 280–A
Waynesville,
North Carolina
28786
(704) 926–0430

MC / V
Moderate

A rustic hewn-log lodge located on a breath-taking mountaintop clearing. The Swag serves meals that are as impressive as the surroundings.

GRANT CORNER INN
Dutch Babies

GRANT CORNER INN
122 Grant Avenue
Santa Fe, New Mexico
87501
(505) 983–6678

MC / V
Expensive

This elegant colonial home is set in one of America's most charming western towns.

¼ *cup butter*
3 eggs
¾ *cup milk*
¾ *cup all-purpose flour*

banana topping (see
following recipe)
2 cups lightly sweetened
whipped cream

Preheat oven to 425°.

Put butter in a large cast-iron skillet and put skillet in hot oven. While butter is melting, beat eggs with electric mixer set at high speed for one minute. Whisk in milk alternately with flour, just until blended (may be slightly lumpy). Remove hot skillet from oven and pour batter onto melted butter. Bake 20 to 25 minutes or until brown and puffy. Dust with powdered sugar and serve immediately with banana topping and lightly sweetened whipped cream. Serves 4.

BANANA TOPPING
3 ripe bananas
3 tablespoons lemon juice
2 teaspoons cinnamon

pinch of nutmeg
banana brandy

Chop bananas, add lemon juice, cinnamon and nutmeg. Blend in banana brandy to taste.

Grant Corner Inn
Santa Fe, New Mexico

F A I R H A V E N   I N N
Orange Tipsy French Toast

6 eggs, lightly beaten
2 tablespoons light cream
pinch of salt
2 tablespoons Triple Sec
  liqueur
1 tablespoon maple syrup

1 teaspoon grated orange
  rind
½ teaspoon grated nutmeg
1 baguette of French bread,
  thinly sliced

In a bowl, mix together all ingredients except bread slices. Soak bread in liquid mixture until all has been absorbed, turning the slices once. Cook on a hot griddle in cooking oil, turning to brown both sides. Serve with syrup and butter. Serves 6.

T H E   S M I T H   H O U S E
Smith House Banana Fritters

cooking oil
2⅓ cups all-purpose flour
½ teaspoon baking
  powder
½ teaspoon baking soda
½ teaspoon salt

2 eggs
½ cup sugar
two 13-ounce cans
  evaporated milk
12 bananas, peeled and
  quartered

Fill deep fryer with oil 4 to 5 inches deep and preheat oil to 375°.

Sift flour, baking powder, baking soda and salt together. In a separate bowl, beat together eggs and sugar. To egg mixture add milk alternately with sifted dry ingredients. Beat lightly after each addition to form a thin batter. Dip bananas into the batter and then drop them into hot oil. Fry, turning occasionally, until golden brown. Serves 10 to 12.

This batter can also be used for apple fritters: add ½ teaspoon cinnamon and ½ teaspoon nutmeg to batter and substitute peeled apple slices for banana quarters.

LINDEN
1 Linden Place
Natchez, Mississippi
39120
(601) 445–5472

No credit cards
Expensive

An antebellum Southern mansion with a doorway used in the filming of *Gone With the Wind*, the Linden is noted for its outstanding collection of federal-period antique furniture and has been awarded Four Diamonds by Mobil.

L I N D E N

Lil's Eggs from Linden

4 squirts Pam™ vegetable
   cooking spray
4 eggs

4 teaspoons half-and-half
2 tablespoons grated
   cheese

Preheat oven to 450°. Spray 4 muffin tins with Pam™.

Drop a raw egg into each tin. Cover each egg with a teaspoon of half-and-half. Sprinkle grated cheese over the top. Bake for 10 minutes. Gently remove eggs from tin and place on plates. Serves 4.

Lil's Grits from Linden

1 quart water
½ cup regular grits
1 cube beef bouillon

½ stick (4 tablespoons)
   butter
salt to taste

In a saucepan, bring the water to a boil. Stir in the grits, bouillon cube and butter. Cook for 15 to 20 minutes, stirring frequently. Consistency should be slightly thick, but not soupy. Add salt to taste. Serves 4.

Linden
Natchez, Mississippi

E D S O N   H I L L   M A N O R

L'Omelette Homard Forestier (Omelette with Lobster and Mushrooms)

butter
4 ounces sliced mushrooms
salt and pepper, to taste
¼ cup good port
¼ cup heavy cream

1 fresh lobster tail, poached, shelled and diced (approximately 1 cup)
1 ounce clarified butter
2 eggs, lightly beaten
freshly grated Parmesan cheese

Sauté mushrooms in butter. Season with salt and pepper. Stir in port and cream. Reduce by half. Add lobster meat and simmer just until the meat is warmed. To a seasoned omelette pan, add clarified butter. Heat the pan, and add the eggs. Stir briskly with a fork to lighten the omelette as it cooks. Add the warmed lobster mixture to the center of the omelette. Fold the omelette over the mixture, slide onto a serving plate and sprinkle with Parmesan cheese. Serve immediately. Serves 2.

D A I R Y   H O L L O W   H O U S E

Apple-Brie Cheese Omelette

½ apple, peeled, cored and thinly sliced
2½ tablespoons butter
2 eggs, room temperature

2 teaspoons cream or milk
dash of salt and pepper
2 tablespoons diced Brie cheese

Sauté apples in one tablespoon butter in a 5" or 6" omelette pan. Beat together eggs, cream or milk, and salt and pepper until blended but not frothy. Melt remaining butter in omelette pan over high heat until foam begins to recede (but before beginning to color). Pour in egg mixture and prepare omelette, beating to lighten but still allowing it to set on bottom. Fill with sautéed apples and cheese cubes. Fold or roll and slide out of pan onto a heated plate. Serves one.

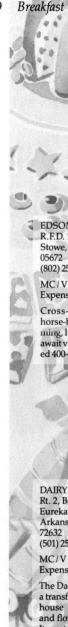

EDSON HILL MANOR
R.F.D. 1
Stowe, Vermont
05672
(802) 253-7371

MC/V
Expensive

Cross-country skiing, horse-back riding, swimming, hiking and barbecues await visitors to this secluded 400-acre country estate.

DAIRY HOLLOW HOUSE
Rt. 2, Box 1
Eureka Springs, Arkansas
72632
(501) 253-7444

MC/V/AE
Expensive

The Dairy Hollow House is a transformed Ozarks farmhouse filled with folk art and flowers in every room. Its restaurant serves "Noveau (sic) Zarks," country cuisine with a French accent.

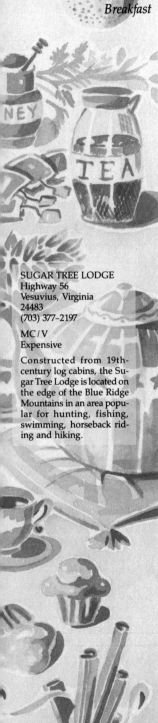

SUGAR TREE LODGE
Highway 56
Vesuvius, Virginia
24483
(703) 377-2197

MC / V
Expensive

Constructed from 19th-century log cabins, the Sugar Tree Lodge is located on the edge of the Blue Ridge Mountains in an area popular for hunting, fishing, swimming, horseback riding and hiking.

S U G A R   T R E E   L O D G E

Super-Duper French Toast

6 eggs	finely grated peel of one
⅔ cup orange juice	orange
⅓ cup Grand Marnier	eight ¾" thick slices French
⅓ cup milk	bread
3 tablespoons sugar	3 to 4 tablespoons butter
¼ teaspoon vanilla	4 tablespoons powdered
¼ teaspoon salt	sugar

The night before, beat eggs in large bowl. Add orange juice, Grand Marnier, milk, sugar, vanilla, salt and orange peel and mix well. Dip bread into mixture, turning to coat all surfaces. Transfer bread to baking dish in a single layer. Pour any remaining egg mixture over top. Cover and refrigerate overnight, turning occasionally, until liquid is absorbed into bread.

In the morning, melt butter in large skillet over medium-high heat. Add bread slices in batches and cook until browned (about eight minutes). Turn and continue cooking another eight minutes, until brown. Cut bread diagonally. Arrange on platter and sprinkle with powdered sugar. Serve immediately with butter and maple syrup. Serves 4.

M A Y H U R S T   B   &   B

Eggs at Mayhurst

4 hard-boiled eggs
2 eggs, beaten lightly
¼ cup cream
pinch of salt
⅛ teaspoon nutmeg

1 tablespoon fresh lemon juice
1 tablespoon butter
2 to 4 English muffin halves
2 to 4 slices Virginia
    country ham

Chop hard-boiled eggs, and set aside. Put beaten eggs, cream, salt, nutmeg and lemon juice in top of double boiler and cook until thick, whisking while cooking. This will take only a few minutes. Do not overcook. Remove from stove, stir in butter until it melts, then stir in chopped eggs. Serve over English muffins topped with Virginia country ham. Serves 2 to 4, depending on appetites.

MAYHURST B & B
P.O. Box 707
Orange, Virginia
22960
(703) 672–5597

MC / V
Moderate

This 36-acre Virginia country estate offers visitors lush rolling pastureland and a fishing pond.

Mayhurst B & B
Orange, Virginia

LA POSADA DE
CHIMAYO
Box 463
Chimayo, New Mexico
87522
(505) 351–4605

No credit cards
Moderate

Guests in this adobe inn experience the traditional lifestyle and beauty of northern New Mexico, as well as a sampling of its spicy cuisine.

LA POSADA DE CHIMAYO

Sofia Trujillo's Red Chili

½ pound diced pork
2 cups water
3 garlic cloves
2 tablespoons fat
2 tablespoons all-purpose
   flour

1 heaping tablespoon ground
   red chili
salt to taste

Bring diced pork, water and garlic to a boil. Lower heat and simmer for about ½ hour, until a nice broth forms. Strain, reserving separately both meat and broth. Melt fat over medium heat. Add flour and cook, stirring, for one minute. Add ground red chile to flour mixture and cook one more minute, stirring constantly. Do not let burn! To the flour-chili mixture add pork broth gradually, stirring constantly; then add the meat. Simmer for 10 to 15 minutes on low heat, stirring occasionally. Salt to taste. Red chili should be the consistency of a thin gravy. Serve over fried eggs with sausage and fried potatoes. Enough for 4 toppings.

HAVENSHIRE INN

North Carolina Applesauce Muffins

½ cup softened butter
1 cup sugar
2 eggs
1 cup unsweetened
   applesauce
1½ teaspoons ground
   cinnamon

1 teaspoon ground allspice
½ teaspoon ground cloves
½ teaspoon salt
1 teaspoon baking soda
2 cups all-purpose flour
½ cup chopped nuts

HAVENSHIRE INN
Route 4, Box 455
Cummings Road
Hendersonville,
North Carolina
28739
(704) 692–4097

MC/V
Moderate to expensive

A 6-room rural retreat on 40 acres overlooking the French Broad River, Havenshire Inn offers hiking, canoeing, fishing and swimming.

Preheat oven to 350°. Butter 24 small muffin tins.

Cream butter and sugar. Add eggs one at a time. Stir in applesauce and spices. Sift together salt, soda and flour. Add to applesauce mixture and beat well. Stir in nuts. Fill muffin tins ⅔ full and bake for 8 to 10 minutes. Batter keeps well in refrigerator, and baked muffins freeze well (reheat before serving). Yields 24 small muffins.

THE REDSTONE INN

Huevos Redstone

½ onion, diced
1 stalk celery, diced
½ green pepper, diced
1½ tablespoons paprika
1½ tablespoons chili powder
½ teaspoon cumin
½ teaspoon black pepper
½ teaspoon salt
½ teaspoon garlic, minced
½ teaspoon oregano

½ teaspoon Cayenne pepper
½ tablespoon chicken base
1 tomato, diced
1 quart water
1 tablespoon cornstarch
8 eggs
8 corn tortillas
2 cups grated cheddar cheese
1 cup sour cream

In a saucepan, sauté onion, celery and green pepper until onions are translucent. Stir in the seasonings, chicken base and diced tomato. Add 3 cups water, bring to a boil and simmer for 20 to 30 minutes. Mix cornstarch with remaining cup of water, add to pan and simmer for another 10 minutes. (This sauce is also great for topping chili rellenos or burritos or as a dip with corn chips.)

Fry eggs. Heat corn tortillas until tender. On an oven-proof serving plate, place 2 tablespoons sauce and cover with a tortilla. Top tortillas with egg and smother with sauce. Top with grated cheese and put under broiler until cheese is melted. Top with sour cream and serve. Serves 8.

THE REDSTONE INN
0082 Redstone Boulevard
Redstone, Colorado
81623
(303) 963–2526

MC / V / AE
Moderate

The historic Redstone Inn was built in 1902 to house miners in a unique village created by a coal baron to prove his theory that people who live in pleasant surroundings are more productive. Today the 35-room inn offers such activities as horseback riding and skiing.

T H E   U N I O N   H O T E L

Sausage

*4 pounds freshly ground
    pork*
¾ tablespoon salt
*½ tablespoon freshly ground
    pepper*

¾ tablespoon powdered sage
*¾ tablespoon fresh ground
    Cayenne pepper*
⅛ cup finely chopped garlic

Mix all ingredients together thoroughly with your hands and
form into 3″ patties. Cook in a skillet until nicely browned.
Serves 20.

Cream Biscuits

*2 tablespoons baking
    powder*
4 cups all-purpose flour
1 teaspoon salt

*¼ pound good quality butter
    (salted, not sweet)*
*1 pint plus 1 tablespoon
    heavy cream*

Preheat oven to 400° (or 425° if your oven is slow). Butter a
baking sheet and set aside. Stir together the first 3 ingredients.
Cut the butter in coarsely. Add the cream gradually. Knead
briefly—just long enough to make a stiff dough. Do not over-
work. Roll out to ½″ thickness. Cut into squares of desired
size. (Cut-dough biscuits hold for 6 hours in the refrigerator.
Do not freeze.) Bake 18 minutes, or until puffed and golden
in color. Serve immediately. Makes 20 biscuits.

THE RUPLEY HOUSE INN

German Coffee Cake

2 cups all-purpose flour
2 cups brown sugar
½ cup butter, chilled
1 egg, lightly beaten
1 cup sour milk or
    buttermilk

1 teaspoon baking soda
1 teaspoon vanilla
cinnamon

Preheat oven to 375°. Butter a square baking pan.

In bowl combine flour, brown sugar and butter, working the butter in until it resembles a coarse meal. Set aside one cup of this mixture for topping. To remainder add beaten egg, sour milk, baking soda and vanilla. Stir to blend. Pour into pan. Crumble topping over batter. Sprinkle a little cinnamon over all. Bake 40 minutes. Serves 8.

The Rupley House Inn
Placerville, California

THE RUPLEY HOUSE INN
Placerville, California 95667
(916) 626-0630

No credit cards
Moderate to expensive

This 50-acre ranch set in the middle of California's gold rush country invites guests to pan for gold, pet the champion quarter horses, and dine on blue-ribbon baked goods.

E L K   C O V E   I N N

Fluffy Two-Cheese Omelette

2 tablespoons butter
5 eggs
¼ cup half-and-half or milk
pepper to taste
2 tablespoons finely chopped
    chives or scallion tops

½ cup grated Tillamook
    cheddar cheese
½ cup grated Turumna
    cheese, or any semi-soft,
    rich white cheese

Preheat oven to 350°.

Heat butter in a heavy skillet. Beat eggs and half-and-half with an electric beater until extremely frothy. Immediately pour into skillet. Sprinkle with pepper and chives. Evenly distribute the 2 cheeses over the top. Cook, tightly covered, about 8 to 10 minutes, or until firm on top. With a spatula, cut the omelette into quarters. Turn 2 quarters over and onto remaining quarters to make 2 separate portions. Serves 2.

Orange Soufflé Omelette

2 tablespoons butter
5 eggs, separated
dash of cream of tartar
1 tablespoon sugar
2 tablespoons all-purpose flour
½ teaspoon baking powder
½ teaspoon dried orange peel
    or lemon peel

½ cup freshly squeezed and
    strained orange juice
1 cup sour cream
1 cup whole berry cranberry
    sauce
garnish of orange slices

Preheat oven to 350°.

Blend sour cream with cranberry sauce and set aside. Melt the butter in a heavy cast-iron skillet. Beat egg whites with cream of tartar and sugar until stiff. Blend the flour, baking powder and orange peel in a bowl. Stir in orange juice and egg yolks and beat until frothy. Gently fold in beaten egg whites. Spread this mixture into the melted butter in the heated skillet. Cook, tightly covered, for about 8 minutes or until just firm. Cut into quarters. Turn each quarter carefully over in place, and cook another 5 minutes. Serve with cranberry-sour cream topping, either between the quarters or on the side. Garnish with orange slices. Serves 2.

ELK COVE INN
P.O. Box 367
Elk, California
95432
(707) 877-3321

No credit cards
Moderate to expensive

Hugging the northern Mendocino coastline, the nine-room Elk Cove Inn is an old-fashioned country establishment serving German and French cuisine.

V E N T A N A   I N N

Eggs Mousseline

Eggs Mousseline is Ventana's sous-chef Peter Charles's favorite egg dish.

6 brioche rolls
6 tablespoons shaved,
  smoked salmon
6 poached eggs
1 cup hollandaise sauce,
  room temperature

1 cup heavy cream, whipped
½ cup chopped fresh dill, or
  to taste

Re-warm brioches. Remove the tops and some of the soft center. Stuff each roll with a tablespoon of shaved smoked salmon and a poached egg. Prepare the mousseline sauce by folding together equal amounts of hollandaise and whipped cream. Fold in dill. Consistency will continue to resemble that of hollandaise sauce. Ladle sauce over the poached eggs in brioches.

Chef Charles suggests serving a sautéed tomato and spinach mixture on the side: He sautés tomato slices quickly on a clean griddle top and serves three per person. He prepares the spinach by melting clarified butter in a sauté pan, throwing in a pinch of minced garlic, and adding one handful per person of washed whole spinach leaves. Spinach is cooked just long enough to wilt. Serves 6.

VENTANA INN
Highway 1
Big Sur, California
93920
(408) 624–4812

All major credit cards
Very expensive

The dramatic California coastline is the setting for this elegant inn and its Mobil four-star restaurant.

THE KENWOOD INN
38 Marine Street
St. Augustine, Florida
32084
(904) 824–2116

MC/V
Moderate

The 15-room, 19th-century Kenwood Inn is located just minutes from the beach in the heart of the oldest city in the United States.

THE KENWOOD INN

Pineapple Bread

3 cups sifted all-purpose
 flour
4½ teaspoons baking powder
1½ teaspoons salt
½ cup sugar

1 egg, lightly beaten
1½ cups milk
4 tablespoons melted butter
1 small can crushed pine-
 apple, well drained

Preheat oven to 350°. Butter a 9½" by 5½" loaf pan.

Sift together flour, baking powder, salt and sugar. Combine egg, milk and melted butter, then add drained pineapple. Pour into flour mixture and stir just enough to moisten dry ingredients—do not beat. Turn into loaf pan and bake 50 to 55 minutes, or until tests done. Makes one loaf or 8 servings (16 slices).

The Kenwood Inn
St. Augustine, Florida

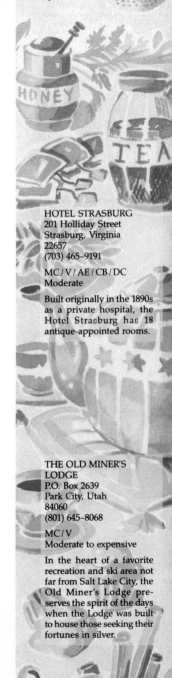

HOTEL STRASBURG

Hotel Strasburg's Fried Tomatoes

3 medium tomatoes, firm
    and not quite ripe
2 cups all-purpose flour
2 teaspoons, more or less,
    garlic powder
1 teaspoon ground cumin
    seed

salt and pepper
1 egg
¾ cup milk
butter

Slice tomatoes into slices ¼″ to ⅜″ wide. Combine flour with seasonings in a shallow bowl. In a separate dish, beat egg, add milk and stir to blend. Dip tomato slices in seasoned flour. Shake off excess flour and dip in egg/milk wash. Dip tomatoes one more time in flour mixture. Allow slices to stand for 10 minutes or more. Sauté in butter for about 2 minutes on each side, or until golden brown. Serves 4 to 6. Serve with either poached or sunny-side-up eggs, country sausage and whole hominy for a breakfast that will carry you through the day.

HOTEL STRASBURG
201 Holliday Street
Strasburg, Virginia
22657
(703) 465-9191

MC/V/AE/CB/DC
Moderate

Built originally in the 1890s as a private hospital, the Hotel Strasburg has 18 antique-appointed rooms.

THE OLD MINER'S LODGE

Miner's Lodge Breakfast

4 large russet potatoes,
    boiled, peeled and cubed
9 pieces bacon, fried crisp
    and crumbled
4 tablespoons butter

½ bell pepper, chopped
minced garlic to taste
salt and pepper
8 eggs, lightly beaten
1 cup grated cheddar cheese

Preheat oven to 350°.

Melt butter in a skillet, add potato cubes and bell pepper and brown slightly. Add garlic to potatoes. Add salt and pepper to taste. Pour eggs over potatoes and cook until eggs form soft curds, stirring constantly. Mix in crumbled bacon. Sprinkle grated cheese over the top. Place skillet in oven or under broiler until cheese is melted. Serves 6.

THE OLD MINER'S
LODGE
P.O. Box 2639
Park City, Utah
84060
(801) 645-8068

MC/V
Moderate to expensive

In the heart of a favorite recreation and ski area not far from Salt Lake City, the Old Miner's Lodge preserves the spirit of the days when the Lodge was built to house those seeking their fortunes in silver.

T H E   A B B E Y

Sly Devil Eggs

6 hard-boiled eggs
¼ cup melted butter
½ teaspoon Worcestershire
    sauce
¼ teaspoon dry mustard
1 (2½ ounce) can deviled
    ham
3 scallions, minced

Preheat oven to 350°. Butter a 9″ casserole dish.

Cut eggs in half and remove yolks. Mix yolks with butter, Worcestershire sauce, mustard, ham and scallions, blending until smooth. Stuff mixture into egg-white halves. Arrange eggs in the casserole.

SAUCE:

¼ cup (½ stick) butter
¼ cup flour
2 cups milk
salt and pepper to taste
English muffins

Melt the butter in a saucepan. Stir in the flour to form a paste and cook for a minute or two. Whisk in the milk and season with salt and pepper. Heat until thickened. Pour the sauce over the eggs and sprinkle with grated cheese. (This can be assembled ahead of time, refrigerated overnight, and heated before serving.)

Bake for 20 to 25 minutes. Serve over toasted English muffins. Serves 6.

THE ABBEY
Columbia Avenue and
Gurney Street
Cape May, New Jersey
08204
(609) 884–4506

MC/V
Expensive

The Abbey, in the historic resort community of Cape May, is located just one block from the Atlantic Ocean.

THE CAPTAIN LORD MANSION

Rick's Soft-Boiled Eggs

Take eggs cold from the refrigerator and poke each with a pin to make a small hole in the large ends. Place eggs in boiling water and boil for 5 minutes. (It is best to use a timer for this!) Remove the eggs and run them under cold water to stop the cooking action. Place each egg in an egg cup and cut off the tops with an egg topper.

Bev's Cranberry Bread

5 cups all-purpose flour	2 eggs
2½ cups sugar	2 cups fresh orange juice
1 teaspoon baking soda	8 tablespoons (1 stick) butter,
3 teaspoons baking	melted
powder	1 cup water
2 teaspoons salt	2 cups cranberries

Preheat oven to 325°. Grease 3 loaf pans and dust with flour.

Sift together flour, sugar, baking soda, baking powder and salt. In a large measuring cup, combine eggs, orange juice, melted butter and water. Make a well in the center of the dry ingredients. Using a whisk or large spoon, stir wet ingredients into well of dry ingredients until all is combined. Fold in cranberries and pour batter into the prepared loaf tins. Bake for one hour, or until bread tests done. Makes 3 loaves.

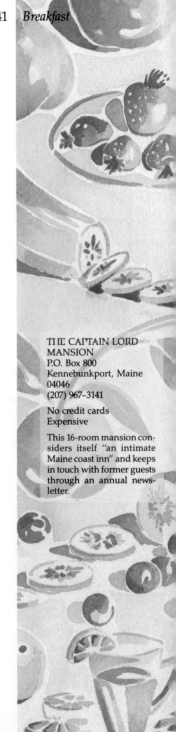

THE CAPTAIN LORD
MANSION
P.O. Box 800
Kennebunkport, Maine
04046
(207) 967-3141

No credit cards
Expensive

This 16-room mansion considers itself "an intimate Maine coast inn" and keeps in touch with former guests through an annual newsletter.

E L   P A R A D E R O

Huevos Rancheros por Gringos

1 large onion, chopped
1 clove garlic, minced
1 tablespoon oil
one 4-ounce can chopped
    green chilies or 3 large
    fresh chilies, skinned and
    chopped
one 32-ounce can stewed
    tomatoes
one 8-ounce can tomato
    sauce
one 6-ounce can tomato paste
1 teaspoon sugar

1 teaspoon vinegar
1 teaspoon chili powder
¾ teaspoon cumin
¾ teaspoon oregano
½ teaspoon salt
½ teaspoon basil
1 bay leaf
freshly ground pepper to
    taste
6 medium-size flour tortillas
6 eggs
1 to 1½ cups shredded jack
    cheese

Preheat oven to 350°.

In large skillet, sauté onion and garlic in oil until limp. Add
chilies, stewed tomatoes, tomato sauce, tomato paste, sugar,
vinegar, chili powder, cumin, oregano, salt, basil, bay leaf and
pepper. Mix well and cover. Let simmer over low heat for at
least 2 hours. If sauce gets too thick, add water. Refrigerate.
At serving time, wrap tortillas in foil and warm while reheat-
ing sauce. Poach eggs. Place warm tortilla on oven-proof plate
and place poached egg in center. Spoon sauce over egg to
cover tortilla. Sprinkle cheese over all and place in oven until cheese is melted. Serves 6.

EL PARADERO
220 West Manhattan
Santa Fe, New Mexico
87501
(505) 988–1177

MC / V
Moderate to expensive

A remodeled 1800 to 1850s
adobe within walking dis-
tance of the plaza, this
12-room inn offers a hearty
full-course breakfast, and
wine and cheese in the afternoon.

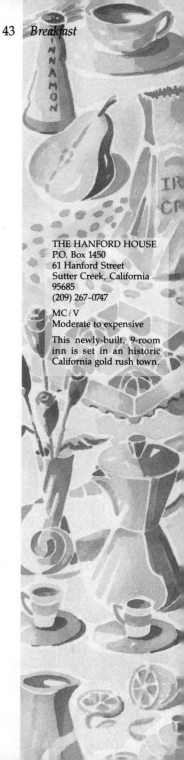

THE HANFORD HOUSE
Jimmy's Favorite Nut Bread

2 large eggs
2 cups brown sugar
3½ cups all-purpose flour
1 teaspoon baking soda

1 teaspoon baking powder
¼ teaspoon salt
1 cup chopped walnuts
1¼ cups buttermilk

Preheat oven to 350°. Butter two loaf pans.

Beat eggs, add sugar and mix well. In a separate bowl, sift together flour, baking soda, baking powder and salt. Stir walnuts into dry ingredients. Add dry ingredients alternately with the buttermilk to egg-sugar mixture. Batter will be stiff. Pour into pans, and level the tops. Bake approximately 50 minutes. Test for doneness. (A cake tester or toothpick should come out dry.) Cool 10 minutes in pans, then turn out onto racks. This heavy nutbread freezes well and is best sliced thin. Also delicious toasted and spread with butter or whipped cream cheese. Each loaf serves 8 to 10.

THE HANFORD HOUSE
P.O. Box 1450
61 Hanford Street
Sutter Creek, California
95685
(209) 267–0747

MC / V
Moderate to expensive

This newly-built, 9-room inn is set in an historic California gold rush town.

The Hanford House
Sutter Creek, California

THE GREY WHALE INN

Apricot-Prune Coffee Cake

This recipe was a blue-ribbon winner at the 1983 Mendocino County (California) Apple Show and Fair.

BATTER:
¾ cup dried apricots
¾ cup pitted dried prunes
3 cups unsifted all-purpose
    flour
½ tablespoon baking powder
¾ teaspoon baking soda
¼ teaspoon salt
¾ cup softened butter
1½ cups sugar
4 eggs

½ tablespoon vanilla
1 cup sour cream
STREUSEL:
½ cup firmly packed light
    brown sugar
2 tablespoons softened butter
2 tablespoons all-purpose
    flour
1 teaspoon cinnamon
2 tablespoons powdered
    sugar (optional)

Preheat oven to 350°. Butter a 10″ tube pan and dust with flour.

Coarsely chop apricots and prunes. Toss to combine. Sift together flour, baking powder, baking soda and salt. Set aside. Beat butter until fluffy (about 3 minutes). Gradually beat in sugar, then eggs, one at a time. Add vanilla. Blend in flour mixture alternately with sour cream, beginning and ending with flour mixture. Blend just until batter is smooth. Gently fold in the prunes and apricots.

Mix together first 4 streusel ingredients with a fork until crumbly. (Will make approximately one cup of streusel.)

Turn ⅓ of the batter into the prepared tube pan, spreading evenly. Sprinkle with ⅓ of the streusel mixture. Repeat, layering the remaining batter and streusel twice. Bake 55 to 60 minutes, or until cake tester comes out clean. Let cool in pan about 20 minutes. Remove from pan to platter. Sift powdered sugar over top if desired. This cake can be served warm. Yields one cake, which serves 10 to 12.

THE GREY WHALE INN
Vanilla Streusel Coffee Cake

3 cups all-purpose flour
1½ teaspoons baking powder
1½ teaspoons baking soda
¼ teaspoon salt
1½ cups softened butter
1½ cups sugar
3 eggs
1½ cups sour cream

1½ teaspoons vanilla
¾ cup firmly packed brown
   sugar
¾ cup chopped nuts
1½ teaspoons cinnamon
2 tablespoons vanilla mixed
   with 2 tablespoons water

Preheat oven to 325°. Butter 10″ tube pan.

Sift together flour, baking powder, baking soda and salt, and set aside. Combine butter and sugar in large bowl and beat until fluffy. Add eggs one at a time, beating well after each addition. Blend in sour cream and vanilla. Gradually add sifted dry ingredients and beat well. Combine brown sugar, nuts and cinnamon in a separate bowl. Turn ⅓ of the batter into the tube pan and sprinkle with ½ of the nut mixture. Repeat. Add remaining batter and spoon diluted vanilla over top. Bake 60 to 70 minutes. Cool completely before removing from pan. (Texture will be moist.) Makes one cake, which serves 10 to 12.

GREY WHALE INN
615 North Main Street
Fort Bragg, California
95437
(707) 964–0640

MC / V / AE
Moderate to expensive

This historic north coast Californian landmark features ocean-view suites, antiques and an extensive art collection.

The Grey Whale Inn
Fort Bragg, California

THE TURNING POINT
Route 23 & Lake Buel
Road
R.D. 2, Box 140
Great Barrington,
Massachusetts
01230
(413) 528-4777

No credit cards
Moderate

Located not far from Tangle-
wood and ski slopes, The
Turning Point has a no-
smoking policy and serves
vegetarian whole-grain
breakfasts.

HAWTHORNE INN
462 Lexington Road
Concord, Massachusetts
01742
(617) 369-5610

No credit cards
Expensive

Located on land that once
belonged to Ralph Waldo
Emerson, the Alcotts and
Nathaniel Hawthorne, the
inn is filled with antique
furnishings, handmade
quilts and sculpture created
by the innkeeper.

THE TURNING POINT

Turning Point Breakfast Muffins

1 cup whole wheat flour
1½ cups raw bran
1 teaspoon baking powder
1 teaspoon baking soda
¾ cup raisins
1 egg, lightly beaten
1 tablespoon oil or melted
   butter

¾ cup milk
¾ cup apple juice
2 tablespoons maple syrup or
   honey
cinnamon to taste
12 walnut halves

Preheat oven to 375°. Butter 12 muffin tins.

Mix together whole wheat flour, bran, baking powder, baking soda and raisins. Add the remaining ingredients, stirring
well to incorporate them evenly. Divide dough into the 12
muffin tins. Top with walnut halves. Bake for about 15
minutes or until muffins test done. Serve hot. Yields 12
muffins.

HAWTHORNE INN

Brown Breakfast Bread

¾ cup honey
¾ cup molasses
3½ cups all-purpose flour
2 teaspoons baking soda
2 teaspoons ginger
2 teaspoons cinnamon

2 teaspoons allspice
dash of salt
2 cups milk
1 cup raisins
2 tablespoons orange
   marmalade

Preheat oven to 350°. Butter a large baking dish.

Beat together honey and molasses. Stir in remaining ingredients until just blended. Bake for 1¼ hours, or until done.

A N C H U C A

Overnight Coffee Cake

¾ cup softened butter
1 cup sugar
2 eggs
1 cup sour cream
2 cups all-purpose flour
1 teaspoon baking powder
1 teaspoon baking soda

½ teaspoon salt
1 teaspoon ground nutmeg
¾ cup firmly packed brown
 sugar
½ cup chopped walnuts or
 pecans
1 teaspoon ground cinnamon

Butter a 13" by 9" by 2" baking pan and lightly dust with flour.

Cream butter and sugar until light and fluffy. Add eggs and sour cream, mixing well. Combine flour, baking powder, baking soda, salt and nutmeg. Add to batter and mix well. Pour into baking pan. In a separate bowl, combine brown sugar, nuts and cinnamon. Mix well and sprinkle evenly over batter. Cover and chill overnight.

In the morning, uncover and bake at 350° for 35 to 40 minutes, or until cake tests done. Serves 15.

S C H W E G M A N N   H O U S E

Coconut Breakfast Bread

2¾ cups all-purpose flour
1¼ cups toasted flaked
 coconut
¾ cup sugar
1 tablespoon baking powder

1 teaspoon salt
1½ cups milk
3 tablespoons melted butter
1 teaspoon coconut extract

Preheat oven to 350°. Butter and flour a 9" by 5" by 3" pan.

Combine flour, coconut, sugar, baking powder and salt in a large bowl and make a well in the center of the mixture. Combine the remaining ingredients. Add the liquids to the dry mixture and stir until well moistened. Spoon into loaf pan. Bake for one hour or until tests done. Cool for 10 minutes in pan, then remove and cool completely on wire rack. Yields one loaf, which serves 8 to 10.

ANCHUCA
1010 First East Street
Vicksburg, Mississippi
39180
(601) 636–4931

MC / V / AE
Very expensive

Guests at Anchuca can immerse themselves in Southern splendor, sipping mint juleps by the swimming pool, relaxing in antique-furnished bedrooms and enjoying breakfast in the inn's magnificent dining room.

THE SCHWEGMANN HOUSE
438 West Front Street
Washington, Missouri
63090
(314) 239–5025

MC / V
Moderate

This pre-Civil War building, with its 9 gracious antique-appointed rooms, sits on the banks of the Missouri River, just an hour's drive west of St. Louis.

S E A F A I R   I N N
Gingerbread Muffins

½ cup sugar
2½ cups all-purpose flour
1½ teaspoons baking soda
1 teaspoon cinnamon
1 teaspoon ginger
½ teaspoon salt

¼ teaspoon nutmeg
1 cup chopped nuts
1 egg
1 cup molasses
1 cup buttermilk
½ cup melted butter

Preheat oven to 350°. Butter muffin tins.

Combine sugar, flour, baking soda, cinnamon, ginger, salt, nutmeg and nuts in a bowl. In a separate bowl, mix egg, molasses, buttermilk and melted butter, and add to the dry ingredients. Stir until just blended. Spoon into muffin tins and bake for 20 to 25 minutes. Test with a toothpick: muffins are done when it comes out clean. Can also be served warmed with whipped cream or ice cream as a dessert. Serves 12.

SEAFAIR INN
14 Shore Road
Box 1221
Ogunquit, Maine
03907
(207) 646–2181

MC / V
Moderate

Nestled in the tiny town of Ogunquit along Maine's rocky southern coast, the classic Seafair Inn has 20 antique-appointed rooms.

Seafair Inn
Ogunquit, Maine

Part 2

B R U N C H

Brunch

This felicitous combination of breakfast and lunch should be slowly savored on a lazy morning. Whether enjoyed in an inn or your own home, the ingredients are the same: good food, pleasant surroundings and good conversation.

The Union Hotel in Benicia (an artist's colony not far from San Francisco) is a mecca for lovers of American cuisine. Brunch guests delight in scrapple, homemade sausage, grits, red plaid hash and scrumptious cream biscuits.

Brunch can be served as individually ordered entrées or as a buffet—a splendid idea for entertaining at home. Gramma's B & B Inn in Berkeley, California, presents so many buffet dishes that it's difficult to decide where to begin. Will it be green salad, crudités, paté, pasta salad, shirred eggs, sausage, home-fried potatoes, or a bit of each? You can greet your guests with a big pitcher of Bloody Marys and then slowly unveil the morning's delights. Whether you serve Shrimp Scampi Bicard, Crustless Quiche, Dill Bread or Buttermilk Pie, it's sure to be a meal to be remembered.

C I T Y   H O T E L

Shrimp-Shirred Eggs

3 tablespoons clarified butter
8 eggs
1 large shallot, chopped
1 cup brut champagne
1½ pounds frozen or fresh
  shrimp, peeled and
  deveined

3 cups heavy cream
¼ pound (1 stick) unsalted
  butter
8 olive rounds
salt and pepper to taste

Preheat oven to 350°. Butter a shallow, oven-proof casserole dish large enough to hold 8 eggs in a single layer.

Crack eggs in the casserole, being careful not to break the yolks. Dot yolks with 1 tablespoon clarified butter and bake uncovered in oven until the yolks are set.

Heat remaining 2 tablespoons clarified butter in a large skillet. Sauté the chopped shallots lightly in the butter. Add champagne and reduce by half. Add the shrimp and cook gently for 2 to 3 minutes. Remove shrimp with a slotted spoon and keep warm. Increase heat under skillet and reduce juices to a thin glaze. Blend in cream and simmer until mixture thickens, about 20 to 30 minutes. Remove from heat and whisk in ¼ pound (1 stick) butter, a tablespoon at a time. Stir in the reserved shrimp, season to taste and pour over the shirred eggs. Garnish with olive slices. Serves 4.

CITY HOTEL
P.O. Box 980
Columbia, California
95310
(209) 532 1479

MC/V
Expensive

Located in an historic gold rush town which is now a state park, the City Hotel's dining room and saloon serve as a training ground for students enrolled in the hotel management and culinary program of a nearby college.

NEW SHERIDAN HOTEL
231 Colorado Avenue
Telluride, Colorado
81435
(303) 728–4351

MC / V / AE
Moderate

The New Sheridan Hotel of
Telluride, a National Historic Landmark, is situated in
one of Colorado's most
beautiful towns.

WHITE CLOUD SYLVAN
RETREAT
Route 447
Newfoundland,
Pennsylvania
18445
(717) 676–3162

MC / V / AE / DC
Inexpensive

This retreat of 50 wooded
acres offers a swimming
pool, tennis court, peace of
mind and meatless natural-
foods cooking.

JULIAN'S AT THE NEW SHERIDAN
Spinach Frittata

2 eggs
½ cup cooked, drained and
    chopped spinach

2 tablespoons water
¼ cup warm tomato sauce
3 strips Mozzarella cheese

Combine eggs, spinach and water. Pour into hot, greased
omelette pan and cook over medium heat until egg mixture
sets. Remove from heat. Ladle sauce over cooked eggs. Place
strips of cheese over top and place under broiler until Mozzarella melts. Serves 2.

WHITE CLOUD SYLVAN RETREAT
White Cloud Cashew Soup

3 cups water or soup stock
1 cup cashew pieces
1 scant teaspoon curry
    powder
1 teaspoon salt

1 heaping teaspoon poultry
    seasoning
4 teaspoons chives for
    garnish
paprika to taste for garnish

Heat first five ingredients to boiling. Put in blender and blend
until smooth. Reheat briefly and serve sprinkled with
chopped chives and paprika. Yields 4 cups or 4 servings.

CAPTAIN MEY'S INN

Quiche Mey

6 eggs
2 cups heavy cream
½ cup fresh bread crumbs
½ teaspoon salt

¼ teaspoon nutmeg
2 tablespoons frozen orange
   juice concentrate
1 cup chopped spinach

Preheat oven to 350°. Butter a quiche dish.

Beat eggs and cream together. Stir in bread crumbs, salt, nutmeg, orange juice and spinach. Pour into quiche dish. Bake 40 minutes in oven or 20 minutes in microwave. Makes one quiche, which serves 8.

CAPTAIN MEY'S INN
R.D. 1, Box 215
Cape May, New Jersey
08204
(609) 884-7793 and
(609) 884-9637

MC/V
Expensive

Named after this resort town's Dutch explorer-founder, the inn keeps the heritage of Holland alive, with a Delft Blue collection, Dutch artifacts and imported cheeses.

Captain Mey's
Cape May, New Jersey

GLENBOROUGH INN
AND COTTAGE
1327 Bath Street
Santa Barbara, California
93101
(805) 966–0589

MC/V
Moderate to very expensive

In the seaside resort community of Santa Barbara, the Glenborough Inn and Cottage has 8 antique-appointed rooms and suites and serves a full breakfast in bed.

GUSTAVUS INN
P.O. Box 60
Gustavus, Alaska
99826
(907) 697–2254

Expensive

A charming Inn with ocean view rooms near Alaska's famous Glacier Bay. The perfect setting for a relaxed getaway.

THE GLENBOROUGH INN
Momma's Egg Casserole

8 slices bread
7 eggs
2½ cups milk
1 teaspoon oregano
½ teaspoon minced garlic
1½ teaspoons salt

4 ounces chopped chilies
3 cups grated sharp
  cheddar
3 cups grated jack cheese
1 avocado, sliced
½ cup sour cream

The night before, place slices of bread in a 9″ by 12″ buttered casserole dish. (Can also be placed in individual casseroles.) Spread the chilies over the bread. Mix together the eggs, milk, oregano, garlic and salt. Pour the egg mixture over the chilies. Sprinkle the cheeses over the entire dish. Cover and refrigerate overnight.

The next morning, preheat oven to 325°. Bake for 50 minutes or until puffy and barely set. (Bake individual casseroles for 15 minutes.) Serve immediately with avocado slices and sour cream garnish. Serves 8 to 12.

GUSTAVUS INN
Halibut or Salmon Parmesan

Preheat oven to 400°. Cut up your cleaned and skinned filets into serving sized pieces, roll in flour, then beaten eggs, then a mixture of 3 parts sourdough bread crumbs (any crumbs will work) and 1 part grated parmesan cheese.

Place on lightly greased open sided cookie sheet and bake at 400° for 15 to 20 minutes. Check for doneness by flaking apart and take out when just done to keep it from drying out. Serve with lemon wedges and cocktail sauce.

HOLIDAY INN

Sherried Crab Quiche

9" pie crust (see following
  recipe)
4 tablespoons softened butter
2 cups heavy cream
4 eggs
1 teaspoon salt
¼ pound shredded Swiss
  cheese

2 tablespoons minced onion
two 6-ounce packages frozen
  snow crab, thawed and
  drained
2 tablespoons dry sherry
⅛ teaspoon Cayenne pepper

Preheat oven to 425°. Prepare pie crust and line a 9" pie plate with the crust. Spread crust with one tablespoon softened butter and set aside.

In a medium bowl, whisk together cream, eggs and salt until well blended. Stir in cheese. Over medium heat, melt remaining 3 tablespoons butter, add the onions and cook until softened (about 5 minutes). Stir onions, crab, sherry and Cayenne pepper into the egg-cream mixture. Pour into buttered pie crust (see following recipe). Bake for 15 minutes. Lower oven to 325° and bake 35 minutes longer, or until knife inserted in center comes out clean. Serves 8.

Butter Pie Crust:
4 tablespoons butter
1 cup unsifted flour

1 egg yolk
5 teaspoons ice water

Cut butter into flour until mixture forms coarse crumbs. Lightly stir in egg yolk with a fork. Add water, a little at a time, and stir until pastry clings together. Form it into a ball and refrigerate for at least one hour before rolling it out.

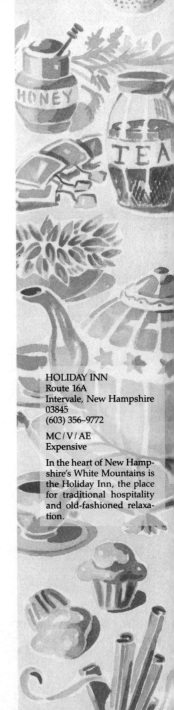

HOLIDAY INN
Route 16A
Intervale, New Hampshire
03845
(603) 356–9772

MC / V / AE
Expensive

In the heart of New Hampshire's White Mountains is the Holiday Inn, the place for traditional hospitality and old-fashioned relaxation.

FOX STAND INN
Route 14
Royalton, Vermont
05068
(802) 763–8437

No credit cards
Inexpensive

The Fox Stand Inn and restuarant is an historic stagecoach stop built in 1818 on the banks of the White River.

BIG YELLOW SUN-
FLOWER
235 Sky Oaks
Angwin, California
94508
(707) 965–3885

No credit cards
Expensive to very ex-
pensive

This small one-suite bed and breakfast located just above northern California's Napa Valley offers a private retreat with very bountiful breakfasts.

F O X   S T A N D   I N N
Eggs à la Jean

This recipe is great for using up leftovers.

2 tablespoons butter	*1 tablespoon sherry*
¼ cup chopped onion	*¼ teaspoon tarragon*
¼ cup cubed baked	*¼ teaspoon basil*
* potatoes*	*salt and pepper to taste*
¼ cup broccoli pieces	*¼ cup cream*
¼ cup diced green pepper	*¼ cup shredded cheddar*
¼ cup ham chunks	* cheese*
1 clove garlic, minced	*8 eggs*

Preheat oven to 350°. Butter a small casserole or 4 boat dishes.

Melt butter in a sauté pan. Sauté onion, potatoes, broccoli, peppers, ham and garlic until heated through. Add sherry and seasonings to taste, then mix in cream and cheese. Stir until cheese melts. Line a casserole or 4 dishes with this mixture, and top with eggs (2 per individual boat dish). Bake until egg whites are firm. Serve this dish with fresh fruit. Serves 4.

B I G   Y E L L O W   S U N F L O W E R   B & B
Sunflower Special

5 eggs	*½ pound jack cheese, grated*
¼ cup all-purpose flour	*¼ cup butter, melted*
½ teaspoon baking powder	*½ cup sour cream*
¼ teaspoon salt	*one 4-ounce can diced green*
½ teaspoon chili powder	* chilies, drained*
1 cup cottage cheese	*sour cream for garnish*

Preheat oven to 350°.

Beat eggs. Add remaining ingredients, beating after each addition. Pour into 6 buttered ramekins. Bake 30 minutes. Serve immediately with a dollop of sour cream. Serves 6.

GRAMMA'S B & B INN

Cauliflower Custard in Swiss Chard Leaves

1 bunch Swiss chard
1 head cauliflower
1 onion, chopped
1 clove garlic, chopped
1½ cups cream or
half-and-half
7 eggs

½ cup grated Parmesan
cheese
½ cup grated mozzarella
cheese
salt, pepper and nutmeg to
taste

Preheat oven to 350°. Butter a ring mold.

Blanch the chard by placing leaves in a large pot of boiling water for a minute or so. Run under cold water, then drain on paper towels. Line ring mold with the leaves of chard, flopping the extra over the outside (you will fold them in later). Chop and cook the cauliflower. While cauliflower is cooking, sauté the onion and garlic. Set aside. Purée cauliflower in a blender or food processor with some of the cream. Add eggs and blend well. Add onion and garlic. Add cheeses, the remaining cream and seasonings. Mix well. Pour custard into the lined mold, lapping the leaves over the top and set pan in a *bain marie* filled with ½" of water. Cover the top of the mold with buttered wax paper. Bake for 25 to 30 minutes or until custard tests done. Loosen edges right away, but allow dish to stand for at least 5 minutes before turning mold out. Can be served hot or cold. Serves 6 to 8.

GRAMMA'S BED &
BREAKFAST INN
2740 Telegraph Avenue
Berkeley, California
94705
(415) 549-2145

MC / V
Expensive

Just a short walk from the University of California campus, Gramma's offers a Sunday champagne brunch.

THE BRIGGS HOUSE

Briggs House Frittata

4 tablespoons butter
1½ cups chopped green
   onions
2 cloves garlic, minced
2 cups finely chopped Swiss
   chard, spinach, broccoli
   or mushrooms
½ teaspoon basil

½ teaspoon oregano
½ teaspoon thyme
12 eggs
1 teaspoon salt
¼ teaspoon pepper
½ cup heavy or sour cream
2 cups shredded Swiss cheese
1 cup Parmesan cheese

Preheat oven to 350°.

Melt butter in a skillet. Sauté green onions and garlic until onion is limp. Add the vegetables and cook until they are just heated through (about 3 minutes). Remove from heat and stir in herbs. Lightly beat the eggs with salt, pepper and cream. Stir in 1½ cups of Swiss cheese and ½ cup Parmesan cheese along with the vegetables. Bake for 30 to 40 minutes. Remove from oven and sprinkle remaining Swiss and Parmesan cheeses over the top. Cook for 5 more minutes to melt the cheese and lightly brown the top. Cool slightly and cut. Serves 8 to 10.

The Briggs House
Sacramento, California

THE BRIGGS HOUSE
2209 Capitol Avenue
Sacramento, California
95816
(916) 441-3214

MC / V / AE
Expensive

Located just a short walk from California's State Capitol building, the elegant Briggs House offers its guests a hot tub, bicycles, complimentary wine and occasional entertainment.

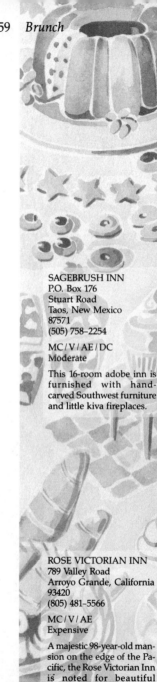

SAGEBRUSH INN
Chili Rellenos

Rellenos may be served as an entrée or as an accompaniment to other Mexican foods.

*enough cooking oil to fill
    deep fryer*
*12 to 16 chilies (fresh or
    canned)*
*½ to ¾ pound mellow cheese,
    such as Colby, Monterrey
    jack, or other mild cheese*
4 cups flour

2 eggs
1½ cups beer
2 cups lukewarm water
½ teaspoon ground cumin
½ teaspoon salt
*½ teaspoon Maggi liquid
    seasoning*
1½ cups flour

Preheat 5 to 6 inches of oil in deep fryer to 350° to 375°.

Split the chilies lengthwise down the top and clean and remove seeds. Cut cheese into strips 4″ long by 1″ wide. Stuff chilies with cheese strips. With an electric mixer, blend flour, eggs, beer, water, cumin, salt and Maggi.

Dip the stuffed rellenos in additional flour, then in the batter. Fry until golden brown. Makes 12 to 16.

ROSE VICTORIAN INN
Cheese Strata

12 slices bread, cubed
2¼ cups grated cheese
3 cups milk
12 eggs
6 tablespoons melted butter

¾ teaspoon dry mustard
chopped ham (optional)
*chopped green chilies
    (optional)*

Preheat oven to 350°. Butter a baking dish.

Layer dish with bread and cheese, ending with cheese. (Chopped ham or green chilies may be layered into the bread and cheese for variety.) Combine milk, eggs, melted butter and mustard in blender for about 10 seconds. Pour over bread/cheese mixture and refrigerate overnight. Bake until firm in the center, about 45 to 60 minutes.

SAGEBRUSH INN
P.O. Box 176
Stuart Road
Taos, New Mexico
87571
(505) 758–2254

MC/V/AE/DC
Moderate

This 16-room adobe inn is furnished with hand-carved Southwest furniture and little kiva fireplaces.

ROSE VICTORIAN INN
789 Valley Road
Arroyo Grande, California
93420
(805) 481–5566

MC/V/AE
Expensive

A majestic 98-year-old mansion on the edge of the Pacific, the Rose Victorian Inn is noted for beautiful gardens and gourmet meals served in the dining room under its crystal chandelier.

THE INN AT WESTON

Salmon Roulade with Dijon Cream or Lemon Curry Sauce

Preheat oven to 400°. Grease a 12″ by 18″ baking pan with 3 tablespoons cooking oil.

ROULADE:

7 eggs
4 tablespoons dried dill weed
¼ cup all-purpose flour

2 tablespoons sour cream
1 extra egg white
dash of cream of tartar

Separate eggs. Mix yolks with dill, flour and sour cream. Set aside. Beat 8 egg whites until fluffy. Add cream of tartar and beat until stiff. Stir some whites into yolk mixture to lighten, then fold in remaining whites. Put baking pan in oven for 5 minutes. Remove pan and spread evenly with egg mixture. Bake for 10 minutes or until it is golden and sides begin to pull away from pan. Cover pan with a clean towel and a baking sheet. Flip pan over so that cake inverts onto towel.

FILLING:

1 pound fresh salmon,
  cooked and flaked
½ cup sour cream

1 cup grated Gruyère cheese
⅓ cup mayonnaise
½ teaspoon salt

Mix salmon, sour cream, grated Gruyère, mayonnaise and salt to make the filling. Spread on cake. Roll cake jelly-roll fashion, using the towel to help. Refrigerate, wrapped tightly in plastic wrap, until ready to use.

SAUCE:

4 tablespoons butter
4 tablespoons all-purpose
  flour
½ cup dry white wine
1 cup fish stock
1 tablespoon Dijon mustard
  (for lemon curry sauce,

substitute 3 to 4 table-
spoons lemon juice and
1½ teaspoons curry
powder)
2 tablespoons fresh chives
½ cup whipping cream

THE INN AT WESTON

Prepare sauce by melting butter and stirring in flour to make a golden-colored roux. Add wine, fish stock, and sauce flavorings (mustard or lemon juice and curry). Cook for 10 to 15 minutes over low heat. Whisk in cream and cook until slightly thickened. Stir in chives and season with salt and pepper.

Before serving, preheat oven to 325°. Remove plastic wrap from roulade and place on buttered baking sheet. Top with some sauce or grated Gruyère cheese. Heat in oven for about 25 minutes or until heated through. Serves 8.

THE INN AT WESTON
Route 100, Box 56
Weston, Vermont
05161
(802) 824–5804

No credit cards
Moderate

The innkeepers at this 13-room inn foster friendships among their guests and prepare creative country cuisine that has been featured in *Gourmet Magazine*.

The Inn at Weston
Weston, Vermont

S N O W V I L L A G E   I N N

Tomato Soup with Cognac

3 pounds ripe tomatoes
  (canned tomatoes may be
  substituted if necessary)
1 large onion
3 ounces butter
1 teaspoon fresh basil or ¼
  teaspoon dried basil

1 pint heavy or whipping
  cream
1 teaspoon brown sugar
4 to 5 tablespoons cognac
salt and pepper to taste

Scald tomatoes and slip off their skins. Chop them coarsely. Chop onion. Melt butter in a large soup pot. Sauté onion till brown and add tomatoes and basil. Let simmer over low heat for one hour. Heat cream and sugar in another pot just until ready to boil. Stirring quickly, pour the cream into the tomatoes. Add cognac, season well with salt and pepper and serve. Serves 6.

Snowvillage Inn
Snowville, New Hampshire

SNOWVILLAGE INN
Stuart Road
Box 176
Snowville,
New Hampshire
03849
(603) 447–2818

All major credit cards
Expensive

This secluded inn offers its guests spectacular views, delicious meals, a friendly atmosphere, tennis, and cross-country ski trails right outside the door.

P E T I T E   A U B E R G E

Crustless Quiche

3 tablespoons butter
2 cups chopped vegetables
  (onions, green pepper,
  broccoli, cauliflower,
  asparagus or other as
  desired)
1 cup grated Swiss cheese

6 eggs
1½ cups heavy cream
½ teaspoon salt
¼ teaspoon pepper
pinch each of nutmeg and
  garlic powder
Parmesan cheese to taste

Preheat oven to 350°. Liberally butter a quiche dish.

Layer vegetables and Swiss cheese in dish halfway to the top. Lightly beat together eggs, cream, salt, pepper and spices. Pour over vegetables and cheese. Bake for 30 minutes. Remove from oven, sprinkle Parmesan cheese on top and return to oven for 15 minutes more.

D U N B A R   H O U S E ,   1 8 8 0

Chili, Cheese, Sausage Trio

two 4-ounce cans whole
  chilies
1 pound link sausages
½ pound Monterrey jack
  cheese
1 pound cheddar cheese
one 13-ounce can
  evaporated milk

2 to 3 tablespoons all-
  purpose flour
1 teaspoon baking powder
8 eggs, beaten lightly
one 8-ounce can tomato
  sauce

Preheat oven to 350°. Butter a 3-quart casserole dish.

Cut chilies into strips. Cook and quarter sausages. Layer chilies, sausages and cheese in the casserole dish. Mix milk, flour, baking powder and beaten eggs and pour over layers. Bake 30 to 40 minutes. Drizzle tomato sauce over and bake 10 minutes more. Let set 10 minutes before cutting and serving. Serves 8 to 10.

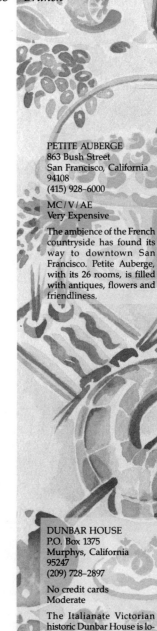

PETITE AUBERGE
863 Bush Street
San Francisco, California
94108
(415) 928–6000

MC / V / AE
Very Expensive

The ambience of the French countryside has found its way to downtown San Francisco. Petite Auberge, with its 26 rooms, is filled with antiques, flowers and friendliness.

DUNBAR HOUSE
P.O. Box 1375
Murphys, California
95247
(209) 728–2897

No credit cards
Moderate

The Italianate Victorian historic Dunbar House is located in a gold rush town in the foothills of the Sierras.

ASA RANSOM HOUSE

Caraway and Sour Cream Soup

4 cups chicken stock
¼ cup chicken fat or ⅛ cup
    butter and ⅛ cup
    cooking oil
2 cups medium-dice onions
1 cup medium-dice celery

1 cup medium-dice carrots
salt and pepper
1 tablespoon caraway seeds
½ cup all-purpose flour
1 cup sour cream
½ cup milk

Heat the chicken stock. In a separate 3-quart saucepan, melt chicken fat or heat butter and oil mixture. Sauté onions, celery and carrots. Season lightly with salt and pepper. Add caraway seeds. Sauté until the onion is transparent. Reduce heat and add flour, stirring constantly so as not to scorch. Cook for 5 to 8 minutes to bind the flour and fat. Gradually add hot chicken stock, stirring to dissolve the roux (mixture of flour and fat). Bring the soup to a boil, then reduce heat and let simmer.

In a separate bowl, mix sour cream with one cup of hot soup and stir vigorously to prevent curdling. Pour this mixture back into the soup and heat, taking care not to allow soup to boil. Finally, add milk and season with salt and pepper to taste. Serve hot. Yields 2 quarts or servings for 8.

ASA RANSOM HOUSE
10529 Main Street
Clarence, New York
14031
(716) 759–2315

No credit cards
Moderate

This 4-room village inn includes a library, gift shop, tap-room and herb garden.

OLDE TOWN FARM LODGE

Carrot Soup

3 tablespoons butter
6 large carrots, peeled and
   sliced
2 medium onions, chopped
1 large potato, peeled and
   diced

4 cups beef broth
½ teaspoon sugar
salt and pepper to taste
parsley or chervil (6 sprigs
    or 3 teaspoons chopped)

Melt butter in a heavy 3-quart saucepan and add carrots, onions and potatoes. Cook over medium heat till lightly browned (about 15 minutes), stirring occasionally. Add beef broth and sugar. Season with salt and pepper to taste. Heat just to boiling point, then reduce heat to low. Cover and cook 15 minutes or until vegetables are tender. Whisk in blender until smooth. Return to saucepan and reheat briefly. Garnish with parsley or chervil. Serves 6.

THE OLDE TOWN
FARM LODGE
Road 4
Box 383B
Chester, Vermont
05143
(802) 875–2346

MC / V / AE
Moderate

This classic Vermont country inn has a pond, a piano and a painstakingly-restored spiral staircase.

LA BORDE HOUSE

Quinney's Bean Soup

1 pound pinto beans, soaked
   in advance
½ cup salt pork, diced
1 cup minced onion
½ cup minced bell peppers
1 tablespoon minced cilantro
   (or coriander), chopped
   fine

1 large tomato, finely
   chopped
1 Serrano pepper, minced
½ tablespoon freshly ground
   black pepper
½ tablespoon ground cumin
3 garlic cloves, minced
salt to taste

Using a 5-quart saucepan, bring beans and salt pork to a boil. Lower to moderate heat and continue cooking for 1½ hours. Stir in onions, bell peppers, tomatoes, cilantro and Serrano pepper. Mix garlic and seasonings together and add to soup. Cook for one more hour, stirring occasionally. Adjust seasonings to taste. Serves 6.

LA BORDE HOUSE
601 East Main Street
Rio Grande, Texas
78582
(512) 487–5101

MC / V / AE
Moderate

Located deep in south Texas, the La Borde House is a blend of old and new, with 8 antique-appointed rooms and 13 in modern style.

THE COLUMNS

Eggplant St. Claire

cooking oil, enough for deep frying
1 cup all-purpose flour
egg wash (5 eggs beaten with small amount of water, a pinch of salt and pepper)
1 cup bread crumbs
4 eggplant halves, peeled and hollowed
2 ounces crabmeat, picked over
1 tablespoon heavy cream
pinch of seafood seasoning
minced garlic to taste
1 cup chopped parsley
1 pint heavy cream

1 pint oyster liquid (canned, if necessary)
chablis or other white wine, to taste
chicken base to taste
pinch of thyme
⅓ cup each of minced green onions, yellow onions, carrots, green bell peppers, celery and turnips
1 teaspoon Worcestershire Sauce
½ cup water
3 tablespoons cornstarch
8 oysters
4 peeled shrimp
chopped parsley for garnish

Fill deep fryer 5 to 6 inches deep with cooking oil. Preheat cooking oil to 320°.

Flour eggplant halves, dip in egg wash and roll in bread crumbs. Deep fry for 5 minutes, turning once. In a saucepan, mix together crabmeat, one tablespoon heavy cream, seafood seasoning (see following recipe), garlic and chopped parsley, and heat until hot. In another saucepan, bring 1 pint heavy cream and oyster liquid to a boil. Add white wine, chicken base, garlic, thyme, green onions, yellow onions, carrots, peppers, celery, turnips and Worcestershire Sauce and continue cooking over low heat. Add water to cornstarch to make a paste. Add cornstarch paste to oyster sauce, stirring over heat until sauce is thickened. Add oysters and shrimp to sauce. Remove from heat. Set deep-fried eggplant on individual plates. Fill each eggplant half with the hot crab filling and top with oyster sauce. Sprinkle with chopped parsley. Make sure each serving includes 2 oysters and 1 shrimp. Serves 4.

T H E   C O L U M N S

SEAFOOD SEASONING:

2½ ounces salt	2 ounces paprika
1 ounce thyme	2 ounces granulated garlic
1 ounce oregano	½ ounce Cayenne pepper
¾ ounce black pepper	

Combine all and store in a tightly covered container.

B E D   &   B R E A K F A S T ,   I N C .

Red Beans and Rice

In New Orleans, this dish is traditionally served on Monday (washday), because it is slow-cooking and takes little attention on a busy day. It is traditionally served with salad and garlic bread.

1 pound dry kidney beans or other red beans	½ pound salt pork, sliced (or seasoning ham or ham hock)
a splash of oil	8 to 10 cups water
1 large onion, chopped	1 bay leaf
¼ cup celery, minced	salt, pepper and Tabasco to taste
¼ cup chopped bell pepper	4 cups hot cooked rice
3 cloves garlic, minced	

Cover beans in water and soak overnight, or boil 2 minutes and allow to stand for one hour. Drain. In a large cooking pot, sauté the vegetables in oil until soft. Add beans, salt pork or ham, water and bay leaf. Cook 1½ to 2 hours, stirring occasionally, crushing some beans to thicken the liquid. Spoon over rice. Serves 6 to 8.

THE COLUMNS
Box 41
3811 Saint Charles Avenue
New Orleans, Louisiana
70115
(504) 899–9308

MC / V / AE
Expensive

Built in 1883 in the Garden District, The Columns has for years been one of New Orleans' finest small hotels and is listed in the National Register of Historic Places.

BED & BREAKFAST, INC.
1021 Moss Street
Box 52257
New Orleans, Louisiana
70152
(504) 488–4640

No credit cards
Inexpensive to expensive

This reservation service organization specializes in matching its guests with suitable rooms in private guest houses in the New Orleans vicinity. Accommodation possibilities include rooms in a French Quarter house beside a patio and swimming pool, in the home of a writer or artist, and in a residential neighborhood near Lake Pontchartrain.

THE INN AT MANCHESTER

Fresh Crab Casserole

1 pound fresh crab meat
½ teaspoon salt
½ teaspoon pepper
1 tablespoon chopped parsley
1 teaspoon minced onion
1 cup heavy cream or half-
   and-half

1½ cups mayonnaise
4 hard-boiled eggs, cut in
   chunks
2 slices homemade or good
   quality white bread,
   cubed

Preheat oven to 350°. Butter a casserole dish.

Combine first 8 ingredients. Put in casserole. Sprinkle cubes of bread over the top. Bake for 40 to 45 minutes. Serves 4.

Herbed Cream Cheese

1 clove garlic, mashed
8 ounces cream cheese
4 ounces whipped sweet
   butter
⅛ teaspoon pepper

⅛ teaspoon thyme
⅛ teaspoon basil
⅛ teaspoon marjoram
⅛ teaspoon dill
¼ teaspoon oregano

Beat all ingredients together thoroughly. Chill 24 hours.

Remove from refrigerator to soften for easy spreading. Serve with crackers or bagel chips. Serves 4.

The Inn at Manchester
Manchester Village, Vermont

THE INN AT
MANCHESTER
Route 7A
Manchester Village,
Vermont
05254
(802) 362-1793

AE
Moderate

This 15-room inn is in the heart of a popular skiing area, and its swimming pool makes it a summer escape as well. The owner is also the chef.

PARADISE RANCH INN

Paradise Grilled Salmon with Tarragon Mayonnaise

6 salmon steaks (about ½ pound each, cut 1" thick)
2 cups mayonnaise
¼ cup chopped fresh tarragon (or ¼ cup chopped fresh parsley combined with 2 teaspoons crumbled dried tarragon)
3 tablespoons finely minced green or red onion

2 tablespoons fresh lemon juice
2 tablespoons chopped capers
¼ teaspoon pepper
salt to taste
lemon or lime slices or fresh tarragon sprigs for garnish

Combine all ingredients (except salmon and garnishes) in large bowl and blend well. Cover and chill 2 to 24 hours.

Arrange rack over grill or broiler pan about 5 inches from heat source. Brush rack with oil. Preheat coals or broiler.

Place salmon steaks on rack and spread top of each with 2 to 2½ tablespoons tarragon mayonnaise. Broil 6 minutes. Turn fish over on grill, mayonnaise-side down, and spread with another 2 to 2½ tablespoons mayonnaise. Broil 4 to 6 more minutes, until tip of knife pierced into middle of steak near center meets little resistance. (Fish sould be barely opaque with a touch of deeper pink color remaining.) Arrange on serving platter. Garnish with lemon or lime slices or tarragon sprigs. Pass around remaining tarragon mayonnaise. Serves 6.

PARADISE RANCH INN
7000 Monument Drive
Grants Pass, Oregon
97526
(503) 479-4333

All major credit cards
Expensive

This elegant ranch is the ultimate in country comfort. Guests will enjoy the heated swimming pool, lighted tennis courts and fishing ponds or—if they wish to get a taste of life on the ranch—a few hours of doing the chores.

T H E   O L E M A   I N N

Smoked Trout & Celery Root Salad

2 cups grated celery
    root immersed in
    lemon-water bath
one 6-ounce smoked trout*
⅓ cup homemade
    mayonnaise
1 tablespoon plus
    1 teaspoon grated
    horseradish

1 small Red Delicious apple,
    diced and immersed in
    lemon-water bath
¼ teaspoon salt
4 butter lettuce leaves
fresh black pepper
½ small red onion, thinly
    sliced
⅓ cup coarsely-chopped
    toasted pecans

Blanch celery root in a large pot of rapidly-boiling salted water for 45 seconds, then plunge immediately into ice water to stop the cooking process. Drain and chill. Flake trout from the bone and refrigerate. Combine the mayonnaise and horseradish. Drain the diced apple. In a bowl, combine celery root, trout and drained apple. Add salt and toss well. Add mayonnaise. Toss again. Taste, and use more salt if needed (the saltiness of the trout will vary). Arrange on chilled plates lined with butter lettuce leaves. Grind fresh pepper on top of each salad. Garnish with onion slices and a sprinkling of toasted pecans. Serves 4.

*Olema Inn's Drew Spangler uses alderwood-smoked trout.

Dungeness Crab Lasagna

1 pound ricotta cheese
¼ cup sour cream
½ cup minced parsley
1 pound Dungeness crab
    meat, picked over
1 teaspoon salt
3 teaspoons minced garlic
freshly ground pepper

½ pound fresh spinach
    lasagna noodles
1½ cups béchamel sauce
1¼ pound grated Mozzarella
    cheese
1 cup grated Parmesan
    cheese

THE OLEMA INN

Preheat oven to 350°. Butter a 9" by 13" baking pan.

Combine ricotta, sour cream, parsley, crab meat, salt, one tea-spoon minced garlic and a generous amount of pepper, and set aside. Cook pasta in rapidly-boiling salted water, until it is three-quarters cooked. Remove from water and place in cold water until ready to use. Add the remaining 2 teaspoons of garlic to the béchamel sauce.

In the baking pan, layer the lasagna as follows: sauce, pasta, sauce, half of the Mozzarella, pasta, sauce, ricotta, pasta, sauce, remaining Mozzarella and the Parmesan cheese. Cover with foil and bake for 30 minutes. Uncover during the final 10 minutes to brown the top. This may be made ahead and reheated before serving. Serves 12.

THE OLEMA INN
10000 Sir Francis Drake
Boulevard
Box 37
Olema, California
94950
(415) 663–9559

MC/V
Expensive

At the entrance to Point Reyes National Seashore just north of San Francisco, the century-old 3-room Olema is noted for its seafood.

C H A L E T   S U Z A N N E

Shrimp Suzanne with Dill

½ cup sour cream
½ cup mayonnaise
½ cup chopped fresh
   cucumber, peeled and
   seeded
⅓ cup minced onion
1½ tablespoons fresh
   chopped dill
1½ teaspoons lemon juice

garlic to taste
salt and pepper
8 drops Tabasco
¼ teaspoon caraway seeds
1 pound shrimp (25 to 30
   count), cooked, peeled
   and cleaned
bibb lettuce

Mix first 10 ingredients together to make a sauce. Stir in shrimp. Mix well and chill. Serve on a bed of bibb lettuce, either as individual servings or in a lettuce-lined bowl. Serves 4 to 6.

CHALET SUZANNE
P.O. Drawer AC
Lake Wales, Florida
33859–9003
(813) 676–6011

All major credit cards
Expensive

With 30 rooms nestled on a private estate in central Florida, the Chalet Suzanne boasts its own lake, a swimming pool, private airstrip and multi-award-winning restaurant.

THE CROWN HOTEL

Shrimp Scampi Caribbean

2 cups sliced peeled
    tomatoes
1 cup tomato purée
2 teaspoons Italian
    seasoning
salt and pepper to taste
16 to 20 jumbo shrimp
    scampi, peeled and
    cleaned
1 cup seasoned flour
2 tablespoons butter

2 tablespoons chopped bell
    peppers
2 tablespoons chopped onion
1 peach, peeled, pitted and
    roughly chopped
2 pineapple rings, roughly
    chopped
2 jiggers dark rum
12 ounces heavy cream
2 teaspoons Worcestershire
    Sauce

Combine first 4 ingredients in a saucepan and cook over high heat for 10 minutes, or until liquid is cooked off, to make tomates concassées. Leftover tomates concassées will keep, covered, in the refrigerator for several days and freeze well.

Dredge scampi in seasoned flour. Melt butter in shallow pan. Cook scampi in butter for one minute. Remove scampi from pan and keep warm. Add peppers, onions, peach and pineapple to pan. Sauté for one minute. Add rum, cream, 2 tablespoons tomates concassées and Worcestershire Sauce. Simmer a minute longer. Return scampi to pan and bring to a boil. Serve with boiled rice. Serves 2.

Shrimp Scampi Bicard

16 to 20 jumbo shrimp
    scampi, peeled and
    cleaned
1 cup seasoned flour
2 tablespoons butter
2 tablespoons sliced
    mushrooms
2 tablespoons peeled, diced
    tomatoes

2 tablespoons finely diced
    onions
4 ounces dry white wine
4 ounces heavy cream
2 teaspoons curry powder
2 tablespoons peeled,
    chopped mango

THE CROWN HOTEL

Dredge scampi in seasoned flour. Sauté in butter for one minute. Remove from pan and keep warm. Add mushrooms, tomatoes and onions to pan. Sauté for one minute. Stir in remaining ingredients and simmer for another minute. Return scampi to pan. Bring to a boil. Spoon over boiled rice. Serves 2.

PATCHWORK QUILT COUNTRY INN, INC.

Buttermilk Pecan Chicken

¾ cup (1½ sticks) butter
1 cup buttermilk
1 egg, lightly beaten
1 cup all-purpose flour
1 cup ground pecans
¼ cup sesame seeds
1 tablespoon paprika
1 tablespoon salt
⅛ teaspoon pepper
2 to 3½ pounds broiler-fryers, cut up
½ cup pecan halves

Preheat oven to 350°. Place butter in large shallow roasting pan and melt in oven. Remove and set aside.

In shallow dish mix buttermilk and egg. In medium bowl combine flour, ground pecans, sesame seeds, paprika, salt and pepper. Coat chicken in buttermilk mixture, then in flour mixture. Place in roasting pan, turning to coat all sides with butter, finishing with skin side up. Scatter pecan halves over chicken and bake about 1½ to 1¾ hours, until chicken is deep golden brown. Serves 8.

THE CROWN HOTEL
109 North Seminole Avenue
Inverness, Florida 32650
(904) 344-5555

V / AE / CB / DC
Expensive

The Crown Hotel began as a general store over a century ago and has evolved into a 34-room inn with swimming pool and award-winning restaurant.

PATCHWORK QUILT COUNTRY INN
11748 C.R. #2
Middlebury, Indiana 46540
(219) 825-2417

No credit cards
Moderate

Located in the heart of Amish country, this Hoosier country inn lives up to its name with patchwork quilts on all the beds.

J E N N Y   L A K E   L O D G E

Chilled Poached Salmon with Mayonnaise Sauce

1 cup white wine
4 cups water
1 leek, trimmed, cleaned and
   chopped
2 carrots, peeled and
   chopped into large
   chunks
4 stalks celery, cleaned and
   chopped
12 parsley stems
3 bay leaves
12 whole black peppercorns
1 lemon, sliced
pinch of salt

five 6-ounce salmon fillets,
   skinned and boned
3 ounces German cucumber
   salad (see following
   recipe)
5 leaves Boston lettuce
mayonnaise (see second
   recipe following)
5 hard-boiled eggs
5 lemon slices, dusted with
   paprika
5 parsley sprigs
5 lemon wedges
5 radish roses

In a pot large enough to contain the 5 pieces of salmon in one layer, combine the wine, water, leek, carrots, celery, parsley, bay leaves, peppercorns, lemon and salt to make a court bouillon (a fish-poaching medium). Bring to a simmer and cook for 15 minutes. Immerse the salmon fillets in a single layer in the court bouillon, skin side down, and cover with foil. Simmer (do not boil) for approximately 10 minutes, or until salmon is firm. Take care not to overcook.

When salmon is cooked, place the entire pot on a bed of ice and refrigerate. The salmon and court bouillon must cool together. To serve, place 3 ounces of German cucumber salad (see following recipe) on a leaf of Boston lettuce. Surround a small glass ramekin of mayonnaise (see second recipe following) with a hard-boiled egg cut in 6 slices. Carefully remove the dark brown matter (medial line or nerve), then place one fillet—skin side down—on each of 5 plates. Place a paprika-dusted lemon slice on the salmon. Garnish with a parsley sprig, lemon wedge and radish rose. Serves 5.

JENNY LAKE LODGE

GERMAN CUCUMBER SALAD:

3 cucumbers
¼ cup salt
1 cup sour cream
juice of 1 lemon
pinch of white pepper

dash of Worcestershire
  Sauce
2 green onions, minced
  (optional)

Peel cucumbers and cut lengthwise. Remove the seeds. Cut into ¼" slices. Place in a colander and sprinkle with salt. Allow to drain for 2 hours. Whip sour cream with lemon juice, white pepper and Worcestershire Sauce and green onions, if desired. Blend quickly with cucumber. Season to taste and chill.

MAYONNAISE:

3 egg yolks
juice of 1 lemon
2 pinches of dry mustard

pinch of white pepper
1 pint of salad oil
pinch of salt (optional)

Place yolks, lemon juice, mustard and white pepper in a mixing bowl and beat well. (An electric mixer can be used.) Whisk or mix in salad oil very slowly in a thin, steady stream, beating vigorously and constantly. Adjust seasoning if desired.

JENNY LAKE LODGE
P.O. Box 240
Moran, Wyoming
83013
(307) 733–4647

MC/V/AE
Very expensive

Guests enjoy horseback riding, bicycling and the beauty of some of the Grand Teton National Park's most outstanding scenery.

S T E A M B O A T   I N N

Sharon Van Loan's
Cold Salmon with Mustard Sauce

5 to 10 pounds cleaned whole
    fresh salmon (For fish
    with head and tail, allow
    about 1 pound per
    person.)
2 tablespoons lemon juice
¾ cup mayonnaise
3 to 4 stalks celery with
    leaves, chopped

3 to 4 onion slices
garnishes of lemon wedges,
    cucumber slices and
    parsley sprigs
mustard sauce (see following
    recipe)

Preheat oven to 450°. Oil a large piece of heavy foil.

Rinse and pat salmon dry. Allow to stand at room temperature for 1½ to 2 hours. Blend lemon juice into mayonnaise. Combine mixture with celery and onion and put into the cavity of the fish. Wrap the fish in the oiled foil, place on a large cookie sheet and bake for 10 to 12 minutes per pound, or until the flesh along the backbone is just beginning to lose its translucence. Turn fish over about halfway through baking time. When done, unwrap foil to release steam and allow salmon to cool. Remove skin from exposed side of fish and gently scrape brown matter (nerve and fat tissue) away. Spoon out mayonnaise stuffing and place fish on serving platter surrounded by stuffing. Decorate with lemon wedges, cucumber slices and lots of parsley. Serve with mustard sauce (see following recipe). Serves 6 to 8.

Mustard Sauce:

2 egg yolks
2 tablespoons Dijon
    mustard
1½ teaspoons dry mustard
1 teaspoon salt
dash of Cayenne pepper
2 teaspoons tarragon
    vinegar

¾ cup vegetable oil
1 tablespoon chopped shallots
1 tablespoon sour cream
¼ teaspoon Bovril™ bouillon,
    dissolved in 1 tablespoon
    warm water
3 tablespoons heavy cream

S T E A M B O A T   I N N

Put yolks, mustards, salt and Cayenne into blender jar and blend until very thick. Blend in vinegar. Slowly add vegetable oil with blender running. When thick and well mixed, add shallots, sour cream, dissolved bouillon and cream. Blend and store in refrigerator until ready to use. (May be made up to several days in advance and kept in the refrigerator.)

This amount is adequate for a small fish. For a 10-pound fish, double the recipe.

T H E   H O M E   R A N C H

Sour Cream Crescent Rolls

3 tablespoons active dry yeast	¼ cup sugar
¼ cup lukewarm water	1 teaspoon salt
½ cup butter	2 eggs, lightly beaten
1 cup sour cream	5 to 6 cups flour
	½ cup melted butter

Preheat oven to 250°.

Dissolve yeast in warm water and set aside. Melt butter in saucepan until it bubbles. Remove from heat and set aside. In a large bowl, combine sour cream, sugar and salt. Stir butter into sour cream mixture and heat to lukewarm. Stir into yeast and add eggs. Work in flour. Dough should be somewhat sticky. Cover with plastic and refrigerate 2 to 4 hours. Divide dough into 4 balls. Roll one ball out into a circle, brush with melted butter and cut into 12 sections (like a pizza). Roll sections from wide to narrow tip and curve slightly to form crescents. Place on greased baking sheet. Repeat with remaining balls of dough. Allow to rise one hour. Bake at 350° for 20 minutes. Serves 8.

STEAMBOAT INN
HC 60, Box 36
Idleyld Park, Oregon
97447
(503) 496–3495

MC / V
Moderate

On the Umpqua River in the Cascade Mountains, this favorite Oregon fishing lodge is famous for its hearty fishermen's dinners.

THE HOME RANCH
Box 822K
Clark, Colorado
80428
(303) 879–1780

No credit cards
Very expensive

Located near Steamboat Springs, this ranch caters to cross-country skiers in winter and outdoor enthusiasts in other seasons with horseback riding, hiking and fishing on the Elk River.

SHELTER HARBOR INN

Creamed Lobster and Johnnycakes

4 tablespoons butter
1 teaspoon finely minced
    shallots
4 tablespoons all-purpose
    flour
1 cup fish stock (or bottled
    clam juice), hot
¼ cup Madeira
1 cup heavy cream
⅛ teaspoon nutmeg

⅛ teaspoon salt
⅛ teaspoon freshly ground
    pepper
⅛ teaspoon Cayenne pepper
2 cups lobster meat
    (reserving whole claw
    meat for garnish)
12 johnnycakes (see
    following recipe)

Melt butter in a heavy saucepan. Add shallots and sauté over moderate heat until tender. Stir in flour and cook, stirring constantly for about 2 minutes, without browning. Remove from heat and stir in the hot stock gradually. Return to heat and stir with a wire whisk until smooth and thick. Stir in Madeira and then heavy cream. Season with nutmeg, salt, pepper and Cayenne. Fold in lobster meat (except for reserved claw). Serve creamed lobster over 3 johnnycakes and garnish with claw. Serves 4 to 6.

SHELTER HARBOR INN JOHNNYCAKES:

2 cups white cornmeal
1½ teaspoons salt
2 teaspoons sugar
2 cups boiling water
½ cup milk, scalded
    and still hot

1 egg, lightly beaten
½ cup bacon fat or other
    cooking oil (enough to
    keep griddle greased)

Mix cornmeal, salt and sugar. Add boiling water and milk and mix well. Stir in egg. Drop by tablespoon onto a medium hot, well-greased griddle or heavy frying pan and fry for 5 minutes on each side. Makes 16 to 20 johnnycakes. Serves 4 to 6.

SHELTER HARBOR INN
10 Wagner Road
Route 1
Westerly, Rhode Island
02891
(401) 322–8883

MC/V/AE
Moderate

This 18-room 18th-century farmhouse-turned-B & B inn is noted for its country cooking.

THE LONE MOUNTAIN RANCH

Dill Bread

2 tablespoons active dry
    yeast
½ cup lukewarm water
4 tablespoons minced fresh
    dill weed
2 tablespoons butter
2 cups cottage cheese

4 tablespoons brown sugar
2 tablespoons minced onion
2 teaspoons salt
½ teaspoon baking soda
2 eggs
4½ cups all-purpose flour

Combine yeast and lukewarm water and set aside. Mix together dill and butter. Combine the remaining ingredients to form dough. After the yeast has begun to bubble, work it into the dough, along with the dill butter. Mix in cottage cheese, brown sugar, onion, salt and baking soda mixture. Knead in flour. Knead for 5 minutes or until gluten forms. The dough should be sticky. Allow it to rise until double in size. Punch down. Allow it to rise again until double in size. Preheat oven to 350°. Punch down dough and roll out. Form into 2 loaves. Bake for about 40 to 45 minutes until golden brown. When done, bread will sound hollow when mittened fist is thumped on bottom of pan. Yields 2 loaves, which each yield 16 slices.

LONE MOUNTAIN
RANCH
Box 145
Big Sky, Montana
59716
(406) 995–4644

MC / V / AE
Expensive

These log cabins near Yellowstone National Park are a family favorite for a summer ranch experience or winter ski vacation.

Lone Mountain Ranch
Big Sky, Montana

T H E   M A N S I O N

Roast Leg of Venison

*leg of deer (weights will
    vary)*
salt and pepper to taste
*garlic (one or more cloves,
    depending on size of
    roast)*

*2 pounds sliced bacon (adjust
    quantity to the size of the
    roast)*

Preheat oven to 500°.

Strip all fat from leg of deer. Rub well with salt and pepper.
Place slivers of garlic in each end of the leg and in the center
along the bone. Place in an open roaster. Cover top of the leg
completely with strips of bacon. Put meat thermometer into
the center of the leg, not touching bone. Place roaster in the
oven. After 30 minutes at 500°, reduce heat to 300°. Cook for
about 20 minutes per pound or until desired doneness is
reached. (Internal temperature for medium rare will be 150°.)
Slice and serve hot. Sliced, cooked onions make an excellent
side dish. Serves 2 to 6, depending on the size of the roast.

Wild Ducks with Chestnut Stuffing

4 wild ducks
3½ cups shelled chestnuts
2 cups seedless raisins
¼ cup butter
1 teaspoon salt
dash of pepper

½ cup heavy cream
1 cup bread crumbs
2 minced onions, or to taste
*4 stalks celery, minced, or to
    taste*
½ cup heavy cream

Preheat oven to 350°.

Clean ducks and soak in cold, clear water or in a little soda
water for one hour. Wash and drain.

Prepare the stuffing by boiling the chestnuts in water until
soft. Cook raisins in a little water, and drain. Drain chestnuts,
and put them through a potato ricer or sieve. Add remaining
ingredients with enough heavy cream to bind stuffing and
mix well.

THE MANSION

Stuff ducks with dressing and place them in a roasting pan. Roast for about 1½ hours. During the last 30 minutes of roasting, add ½ cup heavy cream to the pan. Serve with pan juices ladled over duck. Serve one duck per person.

INN AT PHILLIPS MILL

Filet of Salmon Noilly

butter	½ cup Noilly Prat
6 medium shallots, minced	½ cup water
4 fillets of salmon, approximately ¾ pound each	2 tablespoons lemon juice
	4 large white mushroom caps
salt and pepper	8 small potatoes, boiled
2 cups dry white wine	1 small can salmon caviar
1 cup heavy cream	4 fleurons
small bouquet garni	parsley

Preheat oven to 400°. Butter flat rectangular baking dish.

Spread shallots on bottom of dish. Arrange salmon fillets on top and season with salt and pepper. Pour wine and half of cream over salmon, and add bouquet garni. Bake for 20 minutes, or until salmon is somewhat firm to the touch. Remove fillets from dish and keep warm.

Pour cooking juice into saucepan and bring rest of the cream to a boil. Reduce to ⅔ original volume (about 5 minutes). Whisk in Noilly Prat and boil for 2 minutes longer. Whisk sauce to control cooking and to emulsify.

Bring water and lemon juice, with a pinch of salt added, to a boil. Flute mushroom caps with knife and parboil for 5 minutes. Remove from heat and keep warm.

Place salmon fillets on center of a platter. Cover with sauce. On each fillet put one teaspoon salmon caviar and one mushroom cap. Arrange potatoes and fleurons around the edge of platter and garnish with parsley. Serves 4.

THE MANSION
323 S. Central
Richland Center,
Wisconsin
53581
(608) 647–2808

No credit cards
Moderate

The Mansion, an historic 4-room inn skirting Lake Superior in northern Wisconsin, serves exquisite Edwardian luncheons.

INN AT PHILLIPS MILL
North River Road
New Hope, Pennsylvania
18938
Dining: (215) 862–9919
Lodging: (215) 862–2984

No credit cards
Expensive

Guests at this 5-bedroom stone barn will delight in candlelit dinners and the French cuisine which has made this establishment a favorite.

THE VENICE BEACH HOUSE

Elaine's Apple Dumplings

2 cups all-purpose flour
1 teaspoon salt
2 teaspoons baking powder
12 tablespoons (1½ sticks)
    chilled butter
½ cup milk
2 cups sugar
2 cups water
¼ teaspoon cinnamon
¼ teaspoon nutmeg
4 tablespoons butter

6 or 8 small apples, cored
    but not skinned
½ cup brown sugar
½ cup raisins and chopped
    nuts, combined
½ cup granola
1 teaspoon cinnamon
3 or 4 teaspoons butter
1 cup or more sour cream, to
    taste

To prepare the pastry, sift together flour, salt and baking powder. Cut in the chilled butter, add milk and stir just long enough to moisten the flour. Roll dough out on floured board to ¼" thickness and allow to rest for at least ½ hour.

Meanwhile, prepare a syrup of the sugar, water and spices. Simmer for 5 minutes, then add 4 tablespoons butter. Set aside.

Preheat oven to 275°. Butter a jelly roll pan.

Peel and partially core apples, to create a cavity, but do not cut through bottom. Cut pastry into 5" squares (depending on size of apple), and place one apple on each square. Fill the cavity with a mixture of brown sugar, raisins, nuts and cinnamon, and dot with ½ teaspoon butter. Fold corners and pinch all edges together. Repeat with remaining apples. Place one inch apart on the jelly roll pan. Pour syrup over the "dumplings." Bake for 35 minutes. Serve with sour cream. Serves 6 to 8.

THE VENICE
BEACH HOUSE
15 30th Avenue
Venice, California
90291
(213) 823–1966

MC / V / AE
Expensive

An 8-room historic land-mark, The Venice Beach House is not far from the beach and other attractions of this unusual Los Angeles community.

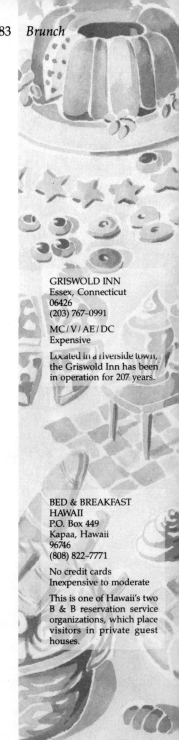

T H E   G R I S W O L D   I N N

Monte Carlo Sandwiches

8 ounces sliced turkey
12 slices white bread, thickly
    buttered (use softened
    butter)

8 ounces sliced ham
4 ounces sliced Swiss cheese
8 eggs, lightly beaten
6 ounces butter

Preheat oven to 350°.

Place ¼ of the sliced turkey on top of one slice of buttered bread. On another slice, put ¼ of the sliced ham and ¼ of the sliced Swiss cheese. Stack the ham and cheese layer on top of the turkey layer. Place the last slice of bread on top (bread will be on the top, in the middle and on the bottom). Repeat with remaining bread, meats and cheese. Cut crust off and cut in half. Wrap sandwiches in plastic wrap and refrigerate until butter has hardened. Dip sandwiches into beaten egg. Melt some butter in a sauté pan and sauté sandwiches a few at a time until browned on both sides. Place in oven and bake for 10 minutes. Serves 4.

GRISWOLD INN
Essex, Connecticut
06426
(203) 767-0991

MC / V / AE / DC
Expensive

Located in a riverside town, the Griswold Inn has been in operation for 207 years.

B E D   &   B R E A K F A S T   H A W A I I

Papaya Seed Dressing

1 teaspoon salt
½ cup sugar
1½ teaspoons dry mustard
1 cup red wine vinegar
2 cups salad oil

2 tablespoons papaya seeds
½ cup chopped macadamia
    nuts
½ onion, minced

In a blender, mix salt, sugar, mustard and vinegar. Add oil gradually with blender running. Remove to a serving bowl. In blender, blend together papaya seeds, macadamia nuts and onion. Stir into oil and vinegar mixture. Best served chilled over any type of tossed greens. Serves 6 or more.

BED & BREAKFAST
HAWAII
P.O. Box 449
Kapaa, Hawaii
96746
(808) 822-7771

No credit cards
Inexpensive to moderate

This is one of Hawaii's two B & B reservation service organizations, which place visitors in private guest houses.

GARRATT MANSION
900 Union Street
Alameda, California
94501
(415) 521-4779

No credit cards
Moderate

In this quiet San Francisco island suburb, guests can bicycle to the beach, observe the harbor life, or stroll down Alameda's shady streets.

G A R R A T T   M A N S I O N

Herbal Popovers

3 eggs
1 cup milk
1 cup all-purpose flour
3 tablespoons butter, melted

1 teaspoon dried thyme, sage
* or crushed basil*
½ teaspoon celery salt

Preheat oven to 450°. Butter eight 6-ounce custard cups.

In blender container, mix eggs, milk, flour, butter, herbs and celery salt. Cover and process at low speed until just smooth. Spoon about ⅓ cup of the batter into each custard cup. Bake for 15 minutes. Reduce heat to 375° and bake for 30 minutes longer or until browned. Serve immediately. Serves 4.

Garratt Mansion
Alameda, California

E D W A R D I A N   I N N

Edwardian Buns

5 to 6 cups all-purpose
   flour
1 cup sugar
2 packages active dry yeast
1 teaspoon salt
¾ cup water

½ cup butter
2 eggs
½ cup cooked mashed
   potatoes
⅛ teaspoon ground nutmeg
melted butter

Combine 1 cup flour sugar, yeast and salt in a large mixing bowl. Stir well. Heat water and butter in a small saucepan (temperature should reach 115° to 120°). Gradually add hot mixture to flour mixture, beating at low speed with an electric mixer until combined. Beat 2 minutes more at medium speed. Beat in eggs, potato, nutmeg and ¾ cup flour and continue beating for an additional 2 minutes. Gradually stir in enough of the remaining flour to make a soft dough. Turn dough out onto a well-floured surface and knead until smooth and elastic (about 10 minutes). Shape into a ball and place in a well-buttered bowl, turning the dough to cover with butter. Cover and allow to rise in a warm, draft-free place for 1½ hours. Punch down and let rise once more, until double in bulk. Divide dough into 12 equal parts. Roll each into a ball and place on buttered baking sheet. Press balls lightly with fingertips to shape them into buns. Cover and allow to rise until double. Brush buns with melted butter. Bake at 375° for 15 to 20 minutes or until golden. Remove immediately. Yields 12.

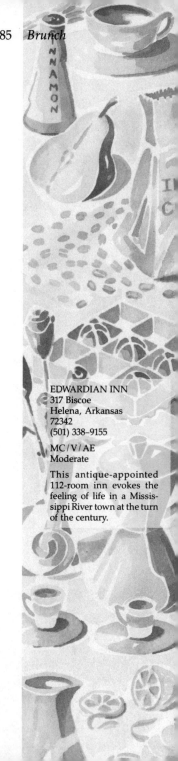

EDWARDIAN INN
317 Biscoe
Helena, Arkansas
72342
(501) 338–9155

MC / V / AE
Moderate

This antique-appointed 112-room inn evokes the feeling of life in a Mississippi River town at the turn of the century.

L O G W O O D   I N N

Aunt Margaret's Pennsylvania Dutch Sticky Buns

1 package active dry yeast
2 cups warm water
    (130°F)
2 tablespoons sugar
5½ to 6 cups all-purpose
    flour
1 egg, beaten
1 teaspoon salt

⅓ cup sugar
1 stick (4 ounces) butter,
    softened
1 cup butter, softened
2 tablespoons sugar
1 teaspoon cinnamon
1½ cup syrup of choice
1 cup walnuts

In a large bowl, dissolve yeast in the warm water and stir until dissolved. Add sugar and 2 cups flour. Beat until smooth. Allow this mixture to stand for 15 to 20 minutes. With a spoon, add the egg, salt, sugar and 4 ounces softened butter. Gradually mix in the remaining flour. Cover with a towel, and allow dough to rise for 1 to 1½ hours in a warm spot. Roll out the dough on a floured board until it is a 15″ by 24″ rectangle. Spread it with 1 cup softened butter, and sprinkle sugar and cinnamon over the top. Roll the dough rectangle lengthwise, and slice it into 1″ slices. Place slices side-by-side into pans which have been buttered and lined with syrup and walnuts. Allow buns to rise another hour. Bake in preheated 400° oven until nicely browned. Makes 12 to 15 buns.

Anadama Bread

According to legend, this delicious bread was invented by an early American fisherman whose wife did not bake. He named his creation after her: Anna, damn her.

7½ to 8½ cups unsifted all-
    purpose flour
2¾ teaspoon salt
2 packages active dry yeast
½ cup butter, softened

2¾ cups warm water
    (130°F)
¾ cup molasses
1¼ cups cornmeal

L O G W O O D   I N N

Combine about 2½ cups flour with salt and yeast. Stir in softened butter. Add water and molasses slowly, blending well. Beat at medium speed with an electric mixer for 2 minutes. Stir in ½ cup flour, and beat at high speed for 2 minutes more. Stir in cornmeal and enough additional flour to form a stiff dough. Turn out onto a floured board and knead until smooth and elastic (about 10 minutes). Place in a large buttered bowl, and butter the top of the dough. Cover and allow it to rise in a warm place until double in bulk (about one hour). Punch down and divide into two parts. Shape dough into 14" by 9" rectangles. Roll the dough up from its short upper end, and seal the sides, folding the sealed ends over and pressing them closed. Place loaves with seam side down in 2 buttered loaf pans. Cover with a towel, and allow them to rise until double in bulk (about 45 minutes). Bake in a preheated oven set at 375° for 40 to 45 minutes or until the loaves sound hollow when tapped. Remove from the pans, and cool on a wire rack. Loaves freeze well.

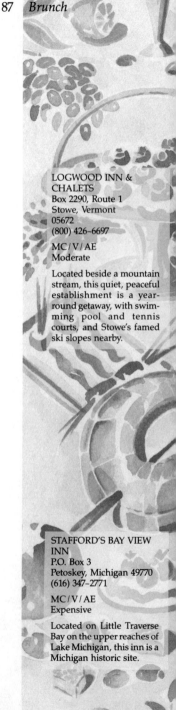

LOGWOOD INN &
CHALETS
Box 2290, Route 1
Stowe, Vermont
05672
(800) 426-6697

MC / V / AE
Moderate

Located beside a mountain stream, this quiet, peaceful establishment is a year-round getaway, with swimming pool and tennis courts, and Stowe's famed ski slopes nearby.

S T A F F O R D ' S   B A Y   V I E W   I N N

Sour Cream Walnut Pie

1 tablespoon butter
⅔ cup brown sugar
1 cup light corn syrup
2 eggs, lightly beaten
1⅔ cups sour cream

2 cups walnuts
2 teaspoons vanilla
¼ teaspoon salt
1 pie crust fitted into
   a pie tin

Preheat oven to 350°.

In a saucepan, heat butter, brown sugar, and corn syrup until all ingredients have liquified. Remove from heat. Combine eggs, sour cream, walnuts, vanilla and salt, and stir into the heated mixture. Return saucepan to stove and cook for 5 more minutes on low heat, stirring constantly to prevent the sour cream and eggs from coagulating. Pour into pie crust and bake for one hour. Serves 8.

STAFFORD'S BAY VIEW
INN
P.O. Box 3
Petoskey, Michigan 49770
(616) 347-2771

MC / V / AE
Expensive

Located on Little Traverse Bay on the upper reaches of Lake Michigan, this inn is a Michigan historic site.

DIE HEIMAT COUNTRY INN

Sauerkraut

2 medium-size heads of
   cabbage

1 teaspoon sugar
2 tablespoons salt

Mix all ingredients thoroughly in a large bowl. Shred then mash cabbage with potato masher until juice collects. Cover bowl with cloth, and let stand for 2 hours. Press kraut into 3 sterilized quart jars as firmly as possible, then fill with the liquid collected in bowl. Fit screw tops loosely so that the kraut can ferment. Let stand at room temperature for several days. Press down again, and if necessary, make a weak salt solution (about 1½ cups salt to one quart water) to fill jars with liquid. Screw tops on tightly and store in a cool place. Sauerkraut is ready to use in 4 weeks. It may be eaten raw as a relish, just as it comes from the jar, or cooked.

Die Heimat Country Inn
Homestead, Iowa

DIE HEIMAT COUNTRY INN

Plain Cooked Sauerkraut

2 cups sauerkraut

2 tablespoons lard

caraway seed (optional)

water to cover

Cook all together for 15 minutes and serve.

Cooked Sauerkraut and Potato

2 cups cooked sauerkraut

1 medium raw potato, grated

Add potato to sauerkraut, cook 10 minutes, and serve.

MOUNT VIEW HOTEL

Orville Knight's Oyster Stew

4 tablespoons butter

1 tablespoon chopped shallots

liquid from oysters plus
    enough clam juice to
    make one quart

2 cups cream

salt and pepper to taste

¼ teaspoon Tabasco

2 tablespoons chopped green
    onions

1 tablespoon chopped red
    pepper

18 oysters, shucked

2 tablespoons grated dry
    cheddar cheese

1 teaspoon grated
    Parmesan

½ teaspoon black caviar for
    garnish

Melt butter in a sauté pan and sauté shallots until they become transparent. Add oyster liquid and clam juice and, over high heat, reduce by ⅔, whisking to prevent overboiling. Add cream and, continuing to whisk over high heat, reduce by ½. Reduce heat and season with salt, pepper and Tabasco. Add green onion and red pepper. Return sauce to a simmer and add oysters. Cook for 5 minutes, taking care not to overcook. Add cheddar cheese and place in an ovenproof soup terrine. Sprinkle with Parmesan cheese and place under broiler, just long enough to brown. Garnish with caviar. Serves 6.

DIE HEIMAT
COUNTRY INN
Homestead, Iowa 52236
(319) 622-3937

MC / V
Inexpensive

This century-old, 19-room inn is in the middle of Iowa's historic Amana colonies.

MOUNT VIEW HOTEL
1457 Lincoln
Calistoga, California
94515
(707) 942-6877

No credit cards
Moderate to expensive

This elaborate 34-room Art Deco inn is located in a popular spa resort at the northern end of the Napa Valley.

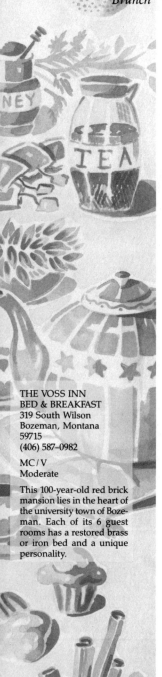

THE VOSS INN
BED & BREAKFAST
319 South Wilson
Bozeman, Montana
59715
(406) 587–0982

MC / V
Moderate

This 100-year-old red brick mansion lies in the heart of the university town of Bozeman. Each of its 6 guest rooms has a restored brass or iron bed and a unique personality.

T H E   V O S S   I N N   B   &   B

Sticky Buns

½ cup sugar
6 cups unsifted all-purpose
    flour
1½ teaspoons salt
2 packages active dry yeast
1 cup milk
⅔ cup water
¼ cup butter
2 eggs, at room temperature

¾ cup melted butter
    (approximately)
½ cup brown sugar
    (approximately)
⅓ teaspoon cinnamon
    (approximately)
¼ cup white sugar
    (approximately)
¼ cup peanut oil
    (approximately)

Spray 4 round cake pans with Pam vegetable cooking spray. Mix 5 cups flour, sugar, salt and yeast. Heat to lukewarm the milk, water and ½ cup butter, and mix them into the flour mixture. Add eggs, working into a dough with your hands (or use the dough hook of an electric mixer). Slowly add last cup of flour. Turn onto a board and knead for 10 minutes. Allow dough to rise in a greased bowl for 20 to 30 minutes. Punch down on a lightly-floured board and roll into a rectangle. Melt the remaining butter. Using a little more than half of the melted butter, cover the bottoms of the 4 round cake pans. Pour the rest of the butter over the dough rectangle, spreading to cover. Sprinkle brown sugar over butter in pans and over the dough rectangle. Combine cinnamon and white sugar and sprinkle over the dough, roll it up, and slice into 24 buns. Place 6 buns in each pan and brush tops with peanut oil. Refrigerate, covered, for 2 to 24 hours.

Preheat oven to 375°. Allow buns to stand at room temperature for 20 to 30 minutes, then bake 25 minutes or until done. Yields 24 sticky buns.

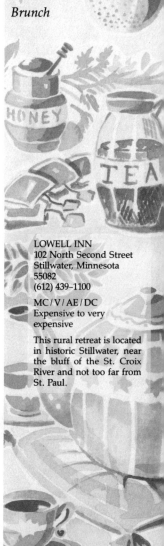

L O W E L L   I N N

Red Cabbage

1 medium-size head of	1½ cups water
red cabbage	1 cup cider vinegar
1 medium-size onion	½ cup sugar
2 large cooking apples	1 teaspoon salt
(approximately	1 bay leaf
1 pound)	2 whole allspice
1 tablespoon bacon fat	6 peppercorns
or butter	1 tablespoon cornstarch

Wash cabbage and remove outer leaves. Quarter cabbage, core and slice. (You should have about 3 quarts.) Slice onion. Pare apples and cut into sixths, removing cores. Toss cabbage, onion and apples together in bacon fat (or butter) which has been melted in a Dutch oven. Add water, cider vinegar, sugar, salt and spices. Simmer uncovered for 20 minutes or until desired tenderness is obtained. Combine cornstarch with a little cold water to make a paste. Add hot cabbage and stir constantly until thickened (about one minute). Makes 8 servings.

Lowell Inn
Stillwater, Minnesota

LOWELL INN
102 North Second Street
Stillwater, Minnesota
55082
(612) 439–1100

MC / V / AE / DC
Expensive to very
expensive

This rural retreat is located in historic Stillwater, near the bluff of the St. Croix River and not too far from St. Paul.

GREENVILLE ARMS

Moravian Orange Rolls

5 to 6 cups unsifted
   all-purpose flour
⅔ cup sugar
1 teaspoon salt
2 packages active
   dry yeast
⅓ cup softened butter
1 cup warm water
   (120° to 130°F)

1 cup mashed potatoes at
   room temperature
2 eggs at room temperature
½ cup softened butter
2 cups firmly packed light
   brown sugar
2 tablespoons orange juice
1 teaspoon ground cinnamon
1 teaspoon grated orange peel

In a large bowl, thoroughly mix 1½ cups flour, sugar, salt and yeast. Stir in ⅓ cup softened butter. Gradually add warm water and beat 2 minutes with an electric mixer at medium speed. Add potatoes, eggs and ½ cup flour. Beat well. Stir in enough additional flour to make a soft dough. Turn out onto lightly-floured board. Knead for 8 to 10 minutes. Place in a greased bowl, turning to grease the top. Cover and allow dough to rise in a warm, draft-free place until doubled in bulk (about one hour).

Greenville Arms
Greenville, New York

G R E E N V I L L E   A R M S

Meanwhile, cream ½ cup butter with brown sugar. Blend in orange juice, cinnamon and orange peel. When doubled, punch down dough. Turn out onto lightly-floured board and divide in half. Roll half of the dough into a 12″ by 18″ rectangle. Spread with half the sugar mixture and roll up like a jelly roll. Seal edges firmly. Slice into 18 equal pieces. Repeat with remaining dough and sugar mixture. Arrange on edge in 4 staggered rows of 9 slices in a buttered 9″ pan. Allow rolls to rise about one hour until they have doubled in size.

Bake at 350° about 30 minutes or until done. Cool on wire racks. Yields 36 rolls.

GREENVILLE ARMS
Greenville, New York
12083
(518) 966–5219

No credit cards
Expensive

The former home of William Vanderbilt in the foothills of the Catskills, the Greenville Arms offers 7 acres of lush lawn, a quaint stream and bridges, gardens and swimming pools for a relaxing weekend getaway.

A U N T   A B I G A I L ' S   B   &   B   INN
Berry Bundt Cake

1½ cups sifted cake flour (not self-rising)	½ cup oat bran
1½ teaspoon baking soda	½ cup chopped almonds
3 tablespoons instant dry nonfat milk	1½ cups sugar
½ teaspoon salt	¾ cup plain yogurt (low fat)
1 teaspoon cinnamon	3 eggs (beaten)
½ teaspoon nutmeg	¾ cup corn oil
½ teaspoon cloves	½ teaspoon orange extract
	1 cup berries of your choice

Preheat oven to 350°. Grease and flour a 12-cup Bundt pan. Mix together the first eight ingredients. Mix in chopped nuts.

In a separate bowl, mix sugar and yogurt. Beat in eggs, corn oil and orange extract. Fold in berries.

Combine wet and dry ingredients, stirring just enough to blend. Pour into prepared Bundt pan. Bake 45–50 minutes. Cool 15 minutes. Serves 12.

AUNT ABIGAIL'S B & B INN
2120 "G" Street
Sacramento, California
95816
(916) 441-5007

Moderate

Ideal for business travelers and romantic escapes, this grand old mansion is in the heart of the State Capitol. Wonderful baked goods and vegetarian food are available. Enjoy!

C A R T E R   H O U S E

Baked Pears Caramel

6 pears

Cut pears in half and core.

Make 4 to 5 slices in pear halves, being careful not to cut all the way through. Butter pan; place pear halves in pan and broil, not too close to flames, for 5 minutes.

SAUCE:

⅔ cup sugar
3 tablespoons cold water
3 tablespoons hot water

1½ cups whipping cream
1 teaspoon vanilla
1 teaspoon well-chilled
unsalted butter

Cook sugar and cold water in sauce pan until sugar melts. Low heat.

Increase heat and bring to boil, brushing sides of pan with wet pastry brush. Boil until syrup becomes light brown. Remove from heat and add hot water. Add cream. Return pan to burner on medium heat and boil until sauce thickens; then add vanilla and butter.

Pour 2 to 3 tablespoons of sauce onto a small, preferably white, dish. Place pear half on top of sauce. Garnish with a mint leaf. Serves 6.

CARTER HOUSE
1033 Third Street
Eureka, California
95501
(707) 442-1390

V / AE / MC
Moderate

The Carter House is a newly built Victorian. The food is truly special. Sumptuous breakfasts are served in a lovely dining room. Let the cordials or tea and cookies send you off to sweet dreams!

R O M E O   I N N
Beer Bagels

2 tablespoons active dry
    yeast
one 12-ounce can of
    beer, at room tem-
    perature

3 tablespoons sugar
1 tablespoon salt
4½ cups all-purpose flour
cornmeal (enough to dust a
    baking sheet)

Dissolve yeast in ½ cup lukewarm beer. Combine remaining beer with sugar and salt. Stir until sugar is dissolved, then add 1 cup flour and yeast mixture. Stir in 3 cups flour to make a stiff dough and knead until smooth (approximately 10 minutes). Cover and let rise in a warm, draft-free place for one hour.

Preheat oven to 375°. Divide dough into 10 pieces and let it relax for 3 minutes. Bring 2 quarts water and 1 tablespoon sugar to a boil. Reduce heat and let simmer. Shape balls into bagels and allow to rest for 10 minutes. Drop bagels into simmering water, 2 or 3 at a time, for 45 seconds, turning once. Remove from water and drain on towel. Place on nonstick baking sheet sprinkled with cornmeal and bake for 30 minutes. Yields 10 bagels.

Romeo Inn
Ashland, Oregon

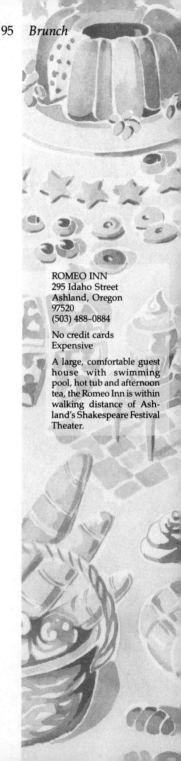

ROMEO INN
295 Idaho Street
Ashland, Oregon
97520
(503) 488–0884

No credit cards
Expensive

A large, comfortable guest house with swimming pool, hot tub and afternoon tea, the Romeo Inn is within walking distance of Ashland's Shakespeare Festival Theater.

EILER'S INN

Apple Strudel

4 to 6 cooking apples, sliced
2 tablespoons sugar
1 tablespoon vanilla
grated rind of 1 orange,
    tangerine or lemon
12 sheets phyllo dough
1½ sticks (12 tablespoons)
    butter, melted

2½ cups bread crumbs (from
    dark, ''interesting''
    breads)
2 cups sugar
2 cups chopped walnuts
¼ cup powdered sugar
1 cup whipped cream
cognac vanilla* to taste

Preheat oven to 350°. Butter a baking dish.

Toss apples with sugar, vanilla and orange rind, and set aside. Place 3 sheets of phyllo dough on a fresh towel and brush with melted butter. Sprinkle heavily with a mixture of one cup each bread crumbs, sugar and walnuts. Place 2 more sheets of phyllo dough onto the first layer and repeat the process. Finally add 2 more sheets of phyllo dough topped with the butter and ½ cup bread crumbs.

Eiler's Inn
Laguna Beach, California

E I L E R ' S   I N N

Place the apples in a row, front to back, on the far right side of the phyllo. Using the towel to help, roll the dough and apples towards the left. Place on a baking sheet and butter the strudel roll well. Bake for about 25 minutes or until golden in color. Place the baked strudel on a board, and slice into pieces. Sift powdered sugar over the roll. Serve with whipped cream laced with cognac vanilla* and sweetened with powdered sugar. Serves 8.

*Kay Tripp of Eiler's Inn prepares her own vanilla by soaking 10 vanilla beans (sliced and scraped) and seeds in a bottle of "the best quality cognac you are willing to buy." The bottle is turned each day and matures in a couple of weeks. As the contents of the bottle dwindle, the mixture can be extended with more beans and cognac.

EILER'S INN
741 South Coast Highway
Laguna Beach, California
92651
(714) 494-3004

MC / V / AE
Very expensive

This inn, built around a courtyard, serves breakfast and afternoon wine and cheese around a fountain.

O A K   S Q U A R E

Old Fashioned Syllabub

Syllabub was served in colonial days as ice cream is now, and is frequently found in cookbooks of the early 18th century.

1½ cups milk	½ teaspoon salt
3 eggs	3 cups light cream
¾ cup sugar	2 cups sweet wine

Scald milk. Beat eggs and add sugar and salt. Gradually mix hot milk into egg mixture and cook over hot water, stirring constantly, until mixture thickens. Cool. Add the light cream and wine and refrigerate. Serve cold in custard cups or glasses. Makes enough for 4 to 6 servings.

OAK SQUARE
1207 Church Street
Port Gibson, Mississippi
39150
(601) 437-4350

MC / V / AE
Expensive

Listed on the National Register of Historic Places, Oak Square is a palatial mansion in a town said by General U.S. Grant to be too beautiful to burn.

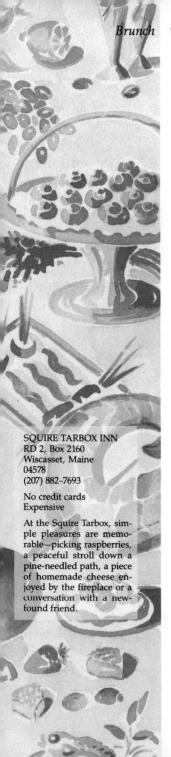

SQUIRE TARBOX INN
RD 2, Box 2160
Wiscasset, Maine
04578
(207) 882-7693

No credit cards
Expensive

At the Squire Tarbox, simple pleasures are memorable—picking raspberries, a peaceful stroll down a pine-needled path, a piece of homemade cheese enjoyed by the fireplace or a conversation with a new-found friend.

THE SQUIRE TARBOX INN

The Squire's Fudge Sauce

¼ pound butter
5 ounces unsweetened baking
   chocolate

1 pound powdered sugar
1 can evaporated milk
1 teaspoon vanilla

Melt together butter and chocolate in double boiler. Add alternately powdered sugar and evaporated milk. Heat over low burner until sauce bubbles and thickens. Add vanilla. Serve over homemade ice cream or mud pie. Makes 3 to 4 cups, which will serve 10 to 12.

Pumpkin-Apple Cake

½ cup butter
1½ cups sugar
2 eggs
2 apples, pared, cored and
   grated
1 cup mashed pumpkin
2 cups all-purpose flour
1 teaspoon baking powder

½ teaspoon baking soda
¼ teaspoon salt
½ teaspoon cinnamon
½ teaspoon nutmeg
¼ teaspoon ground cloves
¼ teaspoon ginger
2 tablespoons powdered
   sugar, or to taste

Preheat oven to 350°. Generously butter a tube or bundt pan and dust lightly with flour.

Cream together butter and sugar with electric mixer. Add eggs one at a time, beating well after each addition. Stir in grated apples and mashed pumpkin. Sift together flour, baking powder, baking soda, salt, cinnamon, nutmeg, ground cloves and ginger. Add to pumpkin mixture, stirring well. Pour into pan and bake for 55 minutes. Cool in pan 10 minutes before turning out cake to cool on a wire rack. When cool, sift powdered sugar over top. Makes one cake which serves 8 to 10.

SUTTER CREEK INN

Apple Oatmeal Crisp

4 cups tart cooking apples,
　peeled and thinly sliced
1½ tablespoons fresh lemon
　juice
3½ tablespoons granulated
　sugar
⅓ cup all-purpose flour

1 cup rolled oats
½ cup firmly packed brown
　sugar
1 teaspoon cinnamon
1 cup chopped walnuts
½ teaspoon salt
½ cup melted butter

Preheat oven to 375°. Generously butter a 9″ square pan.

Combine apples, lemon juice and granulated sugar and put
in pan. In a bowl combine flour, oats, brown sugar, cinnamon, walnuts, salt and melted butter and sprinkle over
apples. Bake for 35 minutes.

SUTTER CREEK INN
P.O. Box 385
Sutter Creek, California
95685
(209) 267–5606

No credit cards
Expensive

This classic California inn is
in a gold rush town popular
for antiquing and sightseeing. The inn features swing-
ing beds which can be
stabilized, and fireplaces in
almost every room.

Sutter Creek Inn
Sutter Creek, California

FLEMING JONES HOMESTEAD

Homestead Baked Apples

*4 apples (Rome, Granny
    Smith or Pippin)*
4 to 16 pieces candied fruit
16 to 24 currants
4 teaspoons butter
*4 teaspoons frozen orange
    juice concentrate*

*4 teaspoons ground
    walnuts*
4 teaspoons cinnamon
4 teaspoons cloves
4 teaspoons sugar
¼ cup water
cream (optional)

Preheat oven to 350°.

Peel apples ⅔ of the way down. Remove stem and core. Rinse apples and place in baking dish. In the inside of each apple place: 2 to 4 small pieces candied fruit, 4 to 6 currants, one teaspoon butter and one teaspoon orange juice concentrate. Sprinkle some ground walnuts, cinnamon, cloves and sugar over the top of each apple. Add a small amount of water to the bottom of the baking dish (the apples themselves will release quite a bit of juice). Cover and bake for 30 to 35 minutes, or until the outsides begin to puff out, sputter and froth. Place each apple in an individual dish. Spoon juice over apples. Serve either hot or cold. Cream may be served on the side. Baked apples may be prepared in advance and reheated. Serves 4.

*The 1883 Fleming Jones Homestead
Placerville, California*

THE FLEMING JONES
HOMESTEAD
3170 Newton Road
Placerville, California
95667
(916) 626–5840

No credit cards
Moderate

Located in the heart of the gold rush country, The Fleming Jones Homestead is a century-old farmhouse, complete with burros, chickens, ducks and a pony.

SPRING BANK FARM INN

Hot Pear Compote

This farm boasts apple, chestnut, walnut and hickory trees. The most bountiful yield, however, comes from 3 aged pear trees whose boughs are heavy with fruit in September and October. These pear recipes are excellent choices for a cool autumn breakfast.

2 cups water	*1 teaspoon cinnamon*
2 tablespoons lemon juice	*8 large pears*
2 tablespoons sugar	*dash of cinnamon*

In a saucepan, bring water, lemon juice, sugar and 1 teaspoon cinnamon to a boil. Peel and halve the pears. Slice into ¼" pieces. Add pear pieces to boiling syrup. Reduce to medium heat and cook until pears soften (about 10 minutes). Serve immediately, topped with a dash of cinnamon. Serves 4.

Pear Butter

2 cups water	*1 teaspoon cinnamon*
2 tablespoons lemon juice	*8 large pears*
2 tablespoons sugar	

Prepare as for the hot pear compote, but continue to cook until the liquid evaporates and the pears turn to a mash. Refrigerate until ready to use. Spread on toast.

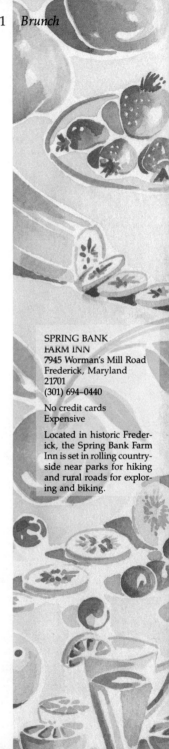

SPRING BANK
FARM INN
7945 Worman's Mill Road
Frederick, Maryland
21701
(301) 694–0440

No credit cards
Expensive

Located in historic Frederick, the Spring Bank Farm Inn is set in rolling countryside near parks for hiking and rural roads for exploring and biking.

THE FOXES BED & BREAKFAST INN

Rhubarb Pie

1½ cups butter
4 cups all-purpose flour
1 tablespoon sugar
1 teaspoon salt
1 egg
1 tablespoon white vinegar
ice water
4 cups rhubarb, cut into ¾''
   lengths

1 cup sugar
2 tablespoons quick-cooking
   tapioca
⅛ teaspoon salt
½ cup seedless raisins
   (optional)
⅛ teaspoon cinnamon
   (optional)

To prepare pastry, work butter into flour, sugar and salt to form pea-sized particles. Drop egg into an 8-ounce cup measure. Add white vinegar and enough ice water to fill the cup. Beat liquids together and add to flour/butter mixture, working the liquid into the solids until the dough forms a ball. Knead lightly on a floured board and roll into separate balls the size of oranges. (This recipe yields more than is needed for a single pie. Freeze the leftover balls and have ready for next time.) Allow the dough to rest, covered, in the refrigerator for at least ½ hour before rolling out 2 separate crusts. Fit one into the bottom of a flour-dusted pie plate. Reserve the other for the top crust.

Preheat oven to 450°.

The Foxes Bed & Breakfast Inn
Sutter Creek, California

THE FOXES BED & BREAKFAST INN

To prepare the pie filling, combine rhubarb, sugar, tapioca and salt. Fill the pie shell with rhubarb mixture. Cut a design for steam vents into the top crust. Brush edge of lower crust with cold water. Place top crust over the pie, and press the edges of both crusts together to seal. Trim excess dough. Flute the rim. Bake for 15 minutes, then reduce heat to 325°, and continue baking for an additional 30 minutes or until the rhubarb is tender. For variety, add seedless raisins and/or a bit of cinnamon to the filling. Yields one pie serving 6 to 8.

THE VILLAGE INN OF WOODSTOCK
Ottauqueechee River Mud Pie

This is the best-selling dessert at The Village Inn.

¼ cup melted butter
1 cup finely-chopped fudge chip cookies (or other favorite cookies)
½ gallon coffee ice cream
fudge sauce (see following recipe)
2 to 3 cups whipped cream

Remove ice cream from freezer to let soften. In a bowl, pour melted butter over cookie crumbs and stir until well blended. In a 9" pie tin, form a crust with the cookie crumb mixture, using your hands or the back of a large spoon. Start with the sides of the pie pan and then press down the bottom. Tamp down the crumbs gently but firmly to keep them in place.

Scoop the softened ice cream into the crust with a large spoon. (The ice cream can start to melt quickly, so work fast or put the ice cream back in the freezer for a few minutes to re-harden.) Gently push the ice cream down to eliminate air pockets. Then smooth around the pie with a cake spatula or knife. Place the pie in the freezer to harden for one hour. Top with your favorite fudge sauce and fresh whipped cream. Serves 8 to 10.

THE FOXES BED & BREAKFAST INN
77 Main Street
P.O. Box 159
Sutter Creek, California 95685
(209) 267-5882

AE
Expensive to very expensive

In the heart of California's gold rush country, this inn delivers a bountiful breakfast to each of its 3 elegant antique-appointed suites: Honeymoon, Anniversary and Imperial.

THE VILLAGE INN OF WOODSTOCK
41 Pleasant Street
Woodstock, Vermont 05091
(802) 457-1255

MC/V
Moderate

This antique-appointed Victorian mansion still contains many of its original furnishings.

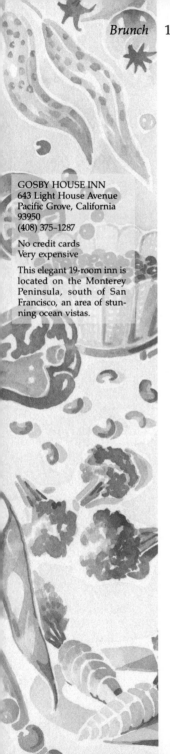

GOSBY HOUSE INN
643 Light House Avenue
Pacific Grove, California
93950
(408) 375-1287

No credit cards
Very expensive

This elegant 19-room inn is
located on the Monterey
Peninsula, south of San
Francisco, an area of stun-
ning ocean vistas.

G O S B Y   H O U S E   I N N

Bread Pudding

6 eggs
2 ½ cups half-and-half
½ cup sugar
cinnamon, mace and
    nutmeg, to taste

¼ teaspoon salt
8 day-old croissants
¾ cup currants or raisins

Preheat oven to 350°. Butter a 10″ pie plate or quiche dish.

Whisk together eggs, half-and-half, sugar, spices and salt.
Pour custard into buttered pan. Break up croissants into bite-
sized pieces and spread over custard. Spread currants on top.
Press croissants and currants lightly into custard. Bake for
about 50 minutes or until it is slightly firm to the touch in the
center. Serves 6 to 8.

Gosby House Inn
Pacific Grove, California

THE GOVERNOR'S INN

Iced Christmas Cherry

3 one-pound cans pitted tart
    cherries (packed in
    water)
2 cinnamon sticks
6 whole cloves
6 whole allspice
1 cup water
½ lemon

½ cup sugar
pinch of salt
1 pint heavy cream
1 tablespoon all-purpose
    flour
2 cups French Medoc wine
sweetened whipped cream for
    garnish

Empty two cans tart cherries and juice into a large pot. Add juice from third can, but reserve cherries. Mix in spices, water, lemon, sugar and pinch of salt. Bring to a boil. In a separate smaller pan, scald cream and whisk in flour. Cool scalded mixture slightly and add to berry mixture. Add wine and bring just to the boiling point. Strain out solids and cool mixture. Add the reserved can of berries and refrigerate. This will keep in the refrigerator for at least 2 weeks.

When ready to serve, place about 5 ounces of chilled potable in a glass bowl or compote—a liner bowl set in crushed ice works well for serving—and garnish with a dollop of whipped cream. Serves 12.

STONE HEDGE INN

Southern Pecan Pie

two 10" pastry-lined
    pie shells
7 eggs
1 quart Karo dark corn syrup

1 cup dark brown sugar
4 ounces (1 stick) butter
1 teaspoon salt
3 cups pecans

Preheat oven to 400°.

Pre-bake pastry shells for 10 minutes. Mix together all ingredients except pecans. Fill each shell with 1½ cups of pecans. Pour filling over pecans and bake 40 minutes or until done. Makes 2 pies, each of which serves 6 to 8.

THE GOVERNOR'S INN
86 Main Street
Ludlow, Vermont
05149
(802) 228–8830

MC/V/AE
Expensive

This southern Vermont small-town B & B is close to 5 lakes, the Black River and Okemo Mountain. Guests sleep soundly in century-old 4-poster brass beds and delight in 4-course gourmet breakfasts.

STONE HEDGE INN
Box 366
Tryon, North Carolina
28782
(704) 859–9114

MC/V
Moderate to expensive

Poised in a beautiful mountain setting on the North-South Carolina border, Stone Hedge Inn has 4 rooms and a swimming pool, and serves memorable meals.

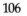

ANNIE'S BED &
BREAKFAST
P.O. Box 928
Big Sandy, Texas
75755
(214) 636–4355

MC / V
Expensive to very
expensive

Annie's Bed & Breakfast is a
unique east Texas Victorian
inn with 13 individually-
decorated rooms and is
home to Annie's Attic, a
national mail-order needle-
craft company.

ANNIE'S BED & BREAKFAST

Italian Coconut Cream Cake

1 cup (2 sticks) softened
   butter
2 cups sugar
5 egg yolks
2 cups all-purpose flour
1 teaspoon baking soda
1 cup buttermilk
1 teaspoon vanilla
one 3½-ounce can coconut

1 cup nuts
5 egg whites, stiffly beaten
5 tablespoons flour
1 cup milk
1 cup sugar
1 cup softened butter
1 teaspoon vanilla
¼ cup coconut

Preheat oven to 350°. Butter and flour 2 cake pans.

Cream butter and sugar. Beat in egg yolks one at a time. Blend in flour combined with baking soda, alternating with buttermilk. Add vanilla. Beat just until smooth. Stir in coconut and nuts. Gently fold in egg whites. Bake for one hour.

To make the frosting, cook 5 tablespoons flour and 1 cup milk on low heat until thick, stirring constantly. Cool. Cream butter, sugar and vanilla. Beat flour mixture into creamed butter mixture until it is creamy and of a spreading consistency.

Frost cake and sprinkle top and sides of cake with coconut. Serves 12 to 14.

W E B B E R   P L A C E

Custard with Berries

3 eggs
⅓ cup brown sugar
½ teaspoon vanilla
2 cups milk, scalded and
   cooled
⅛ teaspoon nutmeg
dash of salt

1 pint fresh berries
½ pint whipped cream,
   slightly sweetened with
   brown sugar
sprinkle of cinnamon
mint sprigs (optional)

Preheat oven to 300°. Butter six 6-ounce custard cups.

Combine eggs, brown sugar and vanilla. Gradually stir in milk. Pour into custard cups and place in 13″ by 9″ by 2″ pan. Pour very hot water into pan to within ½″ of tops of cups. Bake about 45 minutes or until knife inserted between center and edge comes out clean. Remove from water and cool.

Spoon fresh berries and slightly whipped cream on top. Add a dash of cinnamon and sprig of mint for garnish. Serves 6.

WEBBER PLACE
6610 Webber Street
Yountville, California
94599
(707) 944–8384

MC / V
Expensive to very
expensive

The Webber Place is a village inn featuring antique bathtubs and afternoon tea.

The Webber Place
Yountville, California

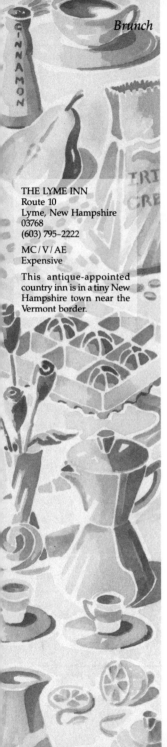

THE LYME INN
Route 10
Lyme, New Hampshire
03768
(603) 795–2222

MC/V/AE
Expensive

This antique-appointed
country inn is in a tiny New
Hampshire town near the
Vermont border.

THE LYME INN

Indian Pudding

2 eggs, lightly beaten
1 cup cornmeal
½ cup all-purpose flour
½ cup molasses
1 teaspoon salt

½ teaspoon ginger
½ teaspoon cinnamon
2 quarts scalded milk
ice cream or whipped cream,
    according to preference

Preheat oven to 350°. Butter a baking dish.

On top of the stove over medium heat, combine all ingredients except the milk and beat thoroughly. Slowly add milk, stirring constantly, until the mixture thickens. Pour into baking dish and bake for 30 minutes. This keeps well in the refrigerator and can be easily heated in a double boiler. Serve warm with ice cream or whipped cream.

The Lyme Inn
Lyme, New Hampshire

TEATIME

Part 3

Teatime

The venerable British tradition of afternoon tea has begun making its appearance on the American scene. Once the preserve of the upper class, it is now enjoying a popularity as an occasion for intimate discussions, informal get-togethers and even business meetings. Although traditionally held between 3:00 and 5:00 P.M., teatime may begin a bit earlier and even run a bit later. Besides tea, such treats as sandwiches, cakes and pastries, crumpets, scones, shortbreads, petit fours and fruits will tempt those who wish to indulge.

For those inns which have adopted the custom, teatime provides a wonderful opportunity for guests and innkeepers to discuss the day's sightseeing and evening dinner plans. At the Mainstay Inn in Cape May, New Jersey, tea is the time when the guests get to know the innkeeper and one another. Guests gather in the dining room or on the veranda or may choose to take their tea and tidbits outside to sit by the garden fountain. Innkeepers say that many a friendship has been cemented over the rim of a teacup.

Each inn has its own special style of serving tea. Ron Gibson, innkeeper of the Victorian Villa in Union City, Michigan, has researched the custom in antique cookbooks and has become an expert in this afternoon affair. To start with, he offers a choice of 30 different teas, including some which he himself blends. To complement the tea, a vast array of delectables are served: perhaps cheese and crackers, meat or cucumber sandwiches, crumpets, smoked fish, scones, tea breads, pastries and fruit. Ron recommends a change of teas midway through the afternoon: maybe starting with a brisk orange pekoe or English breakfast and then switching to an Earl Grey for the sweets.

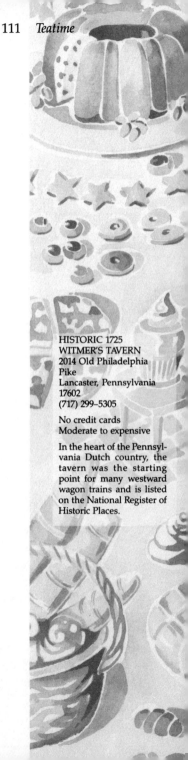

HISTORIC 1725 WITMER'S TAVERN
Lafayette's Rice Cake

General Lafayette acquired his taste for this cake while recuperating in Bethlehem, Pennsylvania, at the Sun Inn during the Valley Forge winter encampment. Wherever he travelled and found Mennonite cooks, he requested it. At Historic 1725 Witmer's Tavern, this dessert is now served on special occasions.

1 cup softened butter	¼ teaspoon nutmeg
2 cups sugar	2 tablespoons rum or brandy
4 egg yolks	1 cup milk
2 cups rice flour	4 egg whites, stiffly beaten
1 cup wheat flour	powdered sugar (optional)
1 teaspoon baking powder	

Preheat oven to 350°. Butter Turk's-head mold (or loaf tin) and lightly dust with flour.

Cream butter and sugar. Add yolks one at a time, beating until creamy. In another bowl, sift rice and wheat flours together with baking powder and nutmeg. Combine rum or brandy with milk in a cup. Blend flour mixture into creamed butter mixture. Gently beat in milk and liquor combination, stopping when a smooth consistency is reached. Fold in beaten egg whites. Transfer to mold and bake for one hour. Cool 15 minutes before removing from pan. Sprinkle powdered sugar over cooled cake, if desired. Yields one cake, which serves 8 to 10.

HISTORIC 1725 WITMER'S TAVERN
2014 Old Philadelphia Pike
Lancaster, Pennsylvania 17602
(717) 299–5305

No credit cards
Moderate to expensive

In the heart of the Pennsylvania Dutch country, the tavern was the starting point for many westward wagon trains and is listed on the National Register of Historic Places.

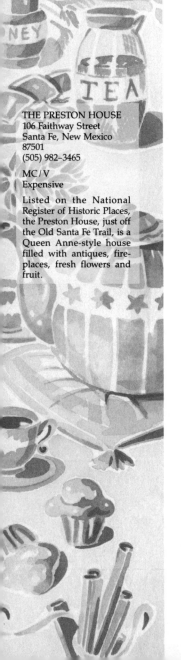

THE PRESTON HOUSE
106 Faithway Street
Santa Fe, New Mexico
87501
(505) 982–3465

MC / V
Expensive

Listed on the National
Register of Historic Places,
the Preston House, just off
the Old Santa Fe Trail, is a
Queen Anne-style house
filled with antiques, fireplaces, fresh flowers and
fruit.

THE PRESTON HOUSE

Scottish Currant Shortbread

⅓ cups currants or raisins
5 tablespoons fresh orange
  juice
1½ cups all-purpose flour

2 tablespoons sugar
½ cup (1 stick) chilled
  unsalted butter

Preheat oven to 350°. Lightly butter baking sheet.

Bring currants or raisins and 4 tablespoons orange juice to boil in small saucepan, stirring. Remove from heat and let cool. Combine flour and sugar in large bowl. Cut in butter till mixture resembles coarse meal. Stir in fruit mixture and remaining tablespoon orange juice. Knead just till dough holds together. Roll dough out on prepared baking sheet into 10" by 12" rectangle. Trim edges and square off corners. Prick surface all over with fork. Sprinkle with sugar. Cut into 24 squares, leaving in place on baking sheet. Bake till pale golden color, 20 to 22 minutes. Re-cut while warm. Cool on rack, then store in airtight container. Yields 24 pieces.

The Preston House
Santa Fe, New Mexico

D E V O N   C O T T A G E

Persimmon Bread

½ cup softened butter
¾ cup sugar
2 eggs
1 cup all-purpose flour
1 cup whole wheat flour
1 teaspoon baking soda
1 teaspoon baking powder
½ teaspoon salt

½ teaspoon ginger
1½ teaspoons cinnamon
1 teaspoon nutmeg
1 cup persimmon pulp
2 teaspoons vanilla
½ cup chopped black
  walnuts

Preheat oven to 375°. Butter a 8" by 4" loaf pan.

Cream butter and sugar. Beat in eggs one at a time and set aside. Sift together flours, baking soda, baking powder, salt, ginger, cinnamon and nutmeg. Gradually blend dry mixture into butter mixture. Add persimmon pulp, vanilla and walnuts, and mix just until a stiff dough forms. Spoon dough into loaf pan. Bake for 50 minutes to one hour or until tests done. Serve sliced, with cream cheese. Yields one loaf, which serves 10 to 15.

L I B E R T Y   I N N   1 8 3 4

Liberty Inn—1834 English Tea Biscuits

1 cup softened butter
2 cups sugar
3 eggs
¾ cup sour cream
1 cup chopped pecans
   (medium-sized pieces)

1 teaspoon vanilla
1 teaspoon baking soda
¼ teaspoon salt
4 cups cake flour

Preheat oven to 425°. Butter a baking dish.

Cream butter and sugar. Add eggs, sour cream, pecans and vanilla, stirring well after each addition. Sift together soda, salt and cake flour. Stir flour mixture into creamed butter and sugar mixture. Place dough on waxed paper and roll into a 1½" rope. Chill or semi-freeze. Cut rope into ¼" slices. Bake 15 to 20 minutes. Cool. Can be stored up to 3 months in airtight canisters. Makes 4 dozen biscuits.

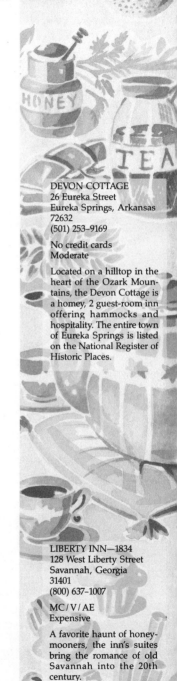

DEVON COTTAGE
26 Eureka Street
Eureka Springs, Arkansas
72632
(501) 253-9169

No credit cards
Moderate

Located on a hilltop in the heart of the Ozark Mountains, the Devon Cottage is a homey, 2 guest-room inn offering hammocks and hospitality. The entire town of Eureka Springs is listed on the National Register of Historic Places.

LIBERTY INN—1834
128 West Liberty Street
Savannah, Georgia
31401
(800) 637-1007

MC / V / AE
Expensive

A favorite haunt of honeymooners, the inn's suites bring the romance of old Savannah into the 20th century.

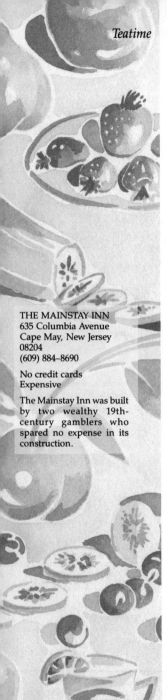

THE MAINSTAY INN
635 Columbia Avenue
Cape May, New Jersey
08204
(609) 884–8690

No credit cards
Expensive

The Mainstay Inn was built
by two wealthy 19th-
century gamblers who
spared no expense in its
construction.

THE MAINSTAY INN

Eccles Cakes

1 ¾ cup all-purpose flour
2 ½ teaspoons baking powder
1 tablespoon sugar
¼ teaspoon salt
¼ cup (½ stick) chilled
   butter

2 eggs
⅓ cup light cream
currants or chopped dates
butter and sugar

Preheat oven to 450°. Butter a baking sheet.

Mix flour, baking powder, sugar and salt together. Work butter into flour mixture to form pea-sized pieces. Beat eggs, and reserve two tablespoons of beaten egg. Stir cream into larger quantity of the eggs. Make a large well in the center of flour mixture. Add egg/cream and stir until just blended. Turn out onto a floured board, and knead until the dough loses its stickiness. Roll out to ¾" thickness, and cut into 2½" rounds. Place 1½" apart on the baking sheet. Poke a hole in the center of each round, and fill with currants or chopped dates. Dot each with butter. Fold opposite edges of circle together, and pinch edges closed like a turnover, sealing in filling. Brush tops with reserved egg and sprinkle with sugar. Bake for 12 minutes. Yields one dozen cakes.

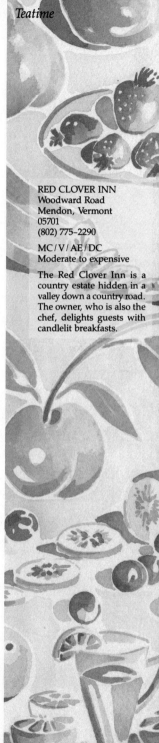

RED CLOVER INN

Poppy Seed Tea Cake

½ pound softened butter
1 cup sugar
4 egg yolks
¼ cup poppy seeds
2 cups cake flour

1 teaspoon baking soda
½ pint (1 cup) sour cream
4 egg whites, stiffly beaten
1 teaspoon almond extract
1 teaspoon cinnamon

Preheat oven to 350°. Butter a tube pan and lightly dust with flour.

Cream together butter, sugar, egg yolks and poppy seeds. Sift together flour and baking soda. Add flour mixture and sour cream alternately to creamed mixture, beginning and ending with flour mixture. Combine egg whites, almond extract and cinnamon and fold into batter. Pour into tube pan. Bake for one hour or until cake tester comes out clean. Cool on cake rack. Serves 8 to 10.

RED CLOVER INN
Woodward Road
Mendon, Vermont
05701
(802) 775-2290

MC / V / AE / DC
Moderate to expensive

The Red Clover Inn is a country estate hidden in a valley down a country road. The owner, who is also the chef, delights guests with candlelit breakfasts.

The Red Clover Inn
Mendon, Vermont

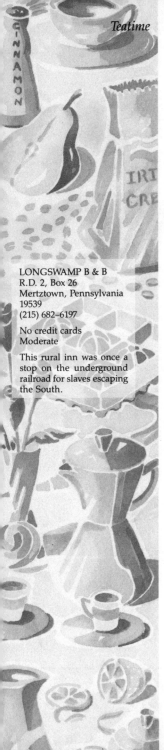

LONGSWAMP B & B
R.D. 2, Box 26
Mertztown, Pennsylvania
19539
(215) 682-6197

No credit cards
Moderate

This rural inn was once a stop on the underground railroad for slaves escaping the South.

LONGSWAMP BED & BREAKFAST

Carrot-Zucchini Bread

2½ cups unsifted all-purpose flour
1 cup unsifted whole wheat flour
1 tablespoon baking powder
1 teaspoon baking soda
½ teaspoon salt
½ cup firmly packed brown sugar
2 eggs

1½ cups buttermilk
2 tablespoons melted butter
grated rinds of 1 orange and 1 lemon
1 cup coarsely shredded zucchini
1 cup coarsely shredded carrots
whipped cream cheese
powdered ginger

Preheat oven to 350°. Butter a 9" by 5" by 3" loaf pan.

Mix together flours, baking powder, soda, salt and sugar. Add remaining ingredients. Stir until well blended. Pour into loaf pan and bake for 1¼ hours or until cake is firm. Cool 5 minutes, then unmold onto a rack. Cool before slicing. When cool, top with whipped cream cheese flavored with a touch of powdered ginger. Yields one loaf, which serves 10.

Longswamp B & B
Mertztown, Pennsylvania

T H E   R A Y   H O U S E

Ray House Lemon Loaf

1 stick (4 ounces) softened
  butter
1 cup sugar
2 eggs
1½ cups bread or all-purpose
  flour
1 teaspoon baking powder

¼ teaspoon salt
1 tablespoon grated lemon
  rind
½ cup milk
lemon sauce (see following
  recipe)

Preheat oven to 350°. Butter and flour a 8½ " by 4½ " loaf pan.

Cream butter and sugar by hand in a large bowl. Add eggs, one at a time, beating after each addition. Sift flour, baking powder and salt onto sheet of waxed paper. With fork, stir in lemon rind. Add flour mixture and milk to batter alternately, beginning and ending with the flour mixture.

Pour into loaf pan. Bake for one hour or until cake tester comes out clean. Pour lemon sauce over hot cake. Allow it to cool for 10 minutes, then turn out on rack to cool completely. Yields one loaf. Keeps for one week when well-wrapped and refrigerated.

LEMON SAUCE:

⅓ cup sugar
¼ cup fresh lemon juice

Stir sugar into lemon juice until it dissolves.

THE RAY HOUSE
83 Hillside Street
Asheville, North Carolina
28801
(704) 252–0106

No credit cards
Moderate

Located in the Blue Ridge Mountain town of Asheville, the 3-room Ray House has the atmosphere of an English country home and a library stocked with lots of good books.

THE WILDWOOD INN
121 Church Street
Ware, Massachusetts
01082
(413) 967-7798

MC / V / AE
Moderate

The Wildwood Inn is a place to relax and unwind—and maybe take a bicycle ride, a plunge in the swimming hole, a hike or a walk down the local shady lanes. Its unusual collection of American primitive antiques and heirloom quilts make it the perfect backdrop for a visit to nearby Old Sturbridge Village.

W I L D W O O D   I N N

Wildwood's Tea Scones

2 cups sifted all-purpose flour	⅓ cup butter
2 tablespoons sugar	1 egg
3 teaspoons baking powder	½ to ¾ cup milk
½ teaspoon salt	1 egg, lightly beaten (optional)

Preheat oven to 425°. Butter a cookie sheet.

Sift flour, sugar, baking powder and salt together. Work in butter until particles are the size of coarse cornmeal. Combine egg and about ½ cup milk. Stir liquids quickly and lightly into the dry ingredients until dough is moistened. The less milk the better, but add a little more if needed, to make a soft dough.

Grease your hands and turn the dough out onto a floured dish towel. Knead gently 15 times. Cut dough in half. Shape each half into a ball and press down to form a round, approximately ¼" thick. Cut each into 8 wedges, like a pie, using a floured knife. Place wedges on a greased cookie sheet or pie tin, without allowing them to touch. Bake for 10 to 15 minutes. If you'd like them to shine, glaze with lightly-beaten egg before baking. Scones should be golden brown when done. Yields 16 scones, which serve 6 to 8.

T A U G H A N N O C K   F A R M S   I N N

Orange Date Bread

rind of 1 orange	1 cup (2 sticks) butter
1 cup water	2 cups all-purpose flour
½ cup chopped dates	2 teaspoons baking powder
¾ cup sugar	½ teaspoon salt
2 tablespoons butter	
1 egg, beaten	

Preheat oven to 350°. Generously butter an 8" by 4" loaf pan.

TAUGHANNOCK FARMS INN

Mix together the first 3 ingredients in a saucepan and boil gently. Add sugar and butter, stir until dissolved and remove from heat. When cooled, stir in remaining ingredients. Put in loaf pan and bake for about 45 minutes or until it tests done. Serve sliced, with cream cheese. Yields one loaf, which serves 8 to 10.

THE NATIONAL HOUSE INN

Sesame Seed Bread or Bars

½ cup sesame seeds
½ cup (1 stick) softened
  butter
1¼ cups all-purpose flour
1 teaspoon baking powder

½ teaspoon salt
1 cup brown sugar
2 eggs
1 teaspoon vanilla

Preheat oven to 375°. Butter 2 small loaf pans.

Toast sesame seeds. Remove from heat. Cream butter and stir in sesame seeds. Sift together flour, baking powder and salt. Beat sugar, eggs and vanilla into butter mixture. Stir in mixture of dry ingredients. Bake in the 2 loaf pans for 25 minutes or until center of loaves test done with a toothpick.

You may also make sesame seed bars by spreading mixture in a greased square pan and baking. Cut into bars while warm. Serves 9 to 12.

The National House Inn
Marshall, Michigan

TAUGHANNOCK
FARMS INN
R.D. 3
Trumansburg, New York
14886
(607) 387-7711

No credit cards
Moderate

The Taughannock Farms Inn is set among some of central New York State's most spectacular scenery: Taughannock Falls and Gorge and Cayuga Lake.

THE NATIONAL HOUSE
INN
102 South Parkview
Marshall, Michigan
49068
(616) 781-7374

MC / V / AE
Expensive

In the historic southern Michigan town of Marshall, the National House Inn has the distinction of being the state's oldest inn.

HEADLANDS INN
P.O. Box 132
Mendocino, California
95460
(707) 937-4431

No credit cards
Expensive

A comfortable restored Victorian home nestled in a northern California village, the Headlands has many rooms with ocean views.

HEADLANDS INN

Headlands Inn Lemon Bread

1 cup softened butter	1 cup buttermilk
2 cups sugar	1 cup chopped nuts
4 eggs	grated rind of 1 lemon
½ teaspoon salt	juice of 3 lemons
½ teaspoon soda	1 cup sugar
3 cups all-purpose flour	

Preheat oven to 350°. Butter and flour two 7″ by 3″ by 2″ loaf pans.

Cream butter and 2 cups sugar. Beat in eggs, one at a time. Sift together salt, soda, and flour, and add alternately, with the buttermilk, to the creamed butter and sugar. Begin and end with the dry ingredients. Fold in the nuts and rind. Bake for 40 minutes to one hour or until tests done.

Heat lemon juice and sugar long enough for the sugar to dissolve. Place warm loaves of bread on foil and spoon juice topping over them. Yields 2 loaves, each of which serves 8.

Headlands Inn
Mendocino, California

C O U N T R Y   I N N

Chocolate Ribbon Cake

½ cup (1 stick) softened
   butter
1 cup sugar
2 cups all-purpose flour
1 teaspoon baking powder
   (double-acting)
1 teaspoon baking soda
1 teaspoon vanilla

one 8-ounce container sour
   cream
2 eggs
½ teaspoon ground
   cinnamon
2 squares semisweet
   chocolate, grated

Preheat oven to 350°. Butter and lightly flour a 9″ by 5″ loaf pan or 10″ bundt pan (a fluted tube cake pan).

In large bowl with mixer at medium speed, beat butter and sugar until light and fluffy. Reduce speed to low. Add flour, baking powder, baking soda, vanilla extract, sour cream and eggs. Beat just until blended, scraping down bowl as necessary. Increase speed to medium, beat one minute, occasionally scraping down bowl. Spread half of the batter evenly in pan. Sprinkle with half of the grated chocolate and ¼ teaspoon cinnamon. Repeat with remaining batter, grated chocolate and cinnamon. Draw knife through batter a few times to swirl chocolate. Bake one hour, or until cake tester inserted in center comes out clean. Cool in pan on wire rack 10 minutes. Serve warm, or let cake cool completely on wire rack and serve at room temperature. Makes one loaf, which serves 16.

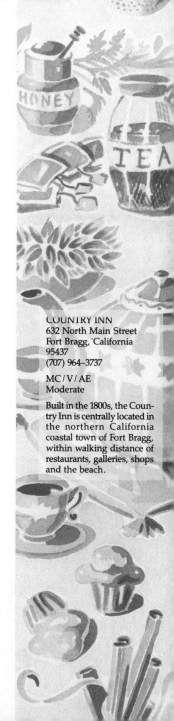

COUNTRY INN
632 North Main Street
Fort Bragg, California
95437
(707) 964–3737

MC / V / AE
Moderate

Built in the 1800s, the Country Inn is centrally located in the northern California coastal town of Fort Bragg, within walking distance of restaurants, galleries, shops and the beach.

VON-BRYAN INN
Route 7, Box 91A
Wears Valley Road
Sevierville, Tennessee
37862
(615) 453–9832

V / MC / AE
Moderate

When staying at the Von-Bryan Inn, one may enjoy the majestic views of the Great Smoky Mountains. The old-fashioned hospitality is enticing and the atmosphere is relaxed. Take time off and enjoy this marvelous Inn.

VON - BRYAN INN
Nut and Honey Crisp

4 cups peeled, sliced apples
¼ cup sugar
1 tablespoon lemon juice
½ cup honey
1 cup all-purpose flour
½ cup packed brown sugar
½ teaspoon salt
½ cup butter or margarine
½ cup chopped nuts

Preheat oven to 375°. Spread apples in a 1½ quart baking dish. Sprinkle with granulated sugar and lemon juice. Pour honey over all.

Mix flour, brown sugar and salt in bowl and work in butter, making a crumbly mixture. Add nuts. Spread over apples and bake for 40 minutes or until apples are tender and crust is crisp and brown.

THE BRITT HOUSE
White Bread

Great for tea sandwiches.

¼ cup butter, melted and
    cooled slightly
1 tablespoon sugar
2 tablespoons yeast
2 teaspoons salt (optional)
2 cups water, lukewarm
up to 6 cups all-purpose
    flour

Combine first 5 ingredients and mix well. Gradually add up to 6 cups flour, a cup at a time, until the dough forms a ball and leaves the sides of the bowl. Turn onto floured surface and knead until dough becomes elastic to the touch, yet is soft as a baby's cheek. Turn into a greased bowl and let rise in warm spot until doubled in bulk. Shape into 2 standard loaves in loaf pans, or divide into eight 3″ by 5″ pans. Let rise again until double. Bake at 350° for 20 minutes or until golden and hollow at the top. Yields 2 loaves, approximately 20 slices each.

T H E   B R I T T   H O U S E

Shortbread

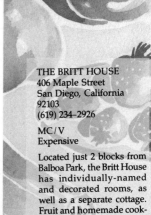

1 pound (4 sticks) softened
  unsalted butter

1 cup sugar
4½ cups all-purpose flour

Preheat oven to 250°. Butter four 9″ pie pans.

Cream together butter and sugar. Add flour, and with hands force mixture together. (A mixer does not work well for this process.) Divide and pat into 4 pie pans. The dough should be about ½″ thick. Pierce in several places with a fork. Score into 16 triangles. (Shortbread is scored raw, then it breaks easily along these lines when baked.) Bake for 1½ to 2 hours, or until slightly golden. Yields 64 pieces.

THE BRITT HOUSE
406 Maple Street
San Diego, California
92103
(619) 234–2926

MC / V
Expensive

Located just 2 blocks from Balboa Park, the Britt House has individually-named and decorated rooms, as well as a separate cottage. Fruit and homemade cookies greet new arrivals, and a formal afternoon tea is served in the parlor.

The Britt House
San Diego, California

PUDING CREEK INN

Sugar Crisp Twisties

1 package active dry yeast
¼ cup lukewarm water
3½ cups sifted all-purpose
  flour
1½ teaspoon salt

1 cup (2 sticks) chilled butter
2 eggs, lightly beaten
½ cup sour cream
3 teaspoons vanilla
1½ cup sugar

Preheat oven to 375°.

Proof yeast in warm water. Sift flour and salt into mixing bowl. Cut in butter until particles are fine. Blend in eggs, sour cream, 1 teaspoon vanilla and yeast. Mix well. Cover and chill at least 2 hours. (Dough may be stored in refrigerator for up to 4 days, shaped and baked as needed.) Combine sugar and 2 teaspoons vanilla. Sprinkle ½ cup on rolling surface. Roll out half the dough on vanilla-sugar mixture to a 16″ by 8″ shape. Sprinkle with about one tablespoon of the vanilla-sugar. Fold one end of the dough over the center, then fold other end to make 3 layers. Turn dough ¼ of the way around, repeat rolling, folding and sprinkling. Roll out to 16″ by 8″. Cut into strips. Twist each strip 2 or 3 times. Place on un-greased cookie sheets. Repeat process with remaining dough and vanilla-sugar mixture. Bake for 15 to 20 minutes until golden brown. Serves 8 to 10.

PUDDING CREEK INN

Cheese Fingers

16 ounces softened cream
cheese
½ cup sugar
4 egg yolks
1 teaspoon vanilla or almond
extract

1 box phyllo dough
½ pound (2 sticks) butter,
melted
chopped almonds (optional)

Preheat oven to 375°.

Blend together cream cheese, sugar, egg yolks and vanilla or
almond extract to make the filling. Unwrap phyllo dough and
cover with damp towel, so that the dough doesn't dry out.
Lay out one sheet of dough and brush with melted butter.
Fold over the top half of the sheet. Brush again with butter.
Put 2 teaspoons of filling at one long end. Take wide ends
and fold ½" in on each side. Starting at filling end, roll up
into a "finger." Brush with butter. Put seam-side down on ungreased cookie sheet. Sprinkle with almonds, if desired.
Repeat with remaining dough and filling. Bake for 10 to 15
minutes, or until brown. Serves 6 to 8.

PUDDING CREEK INN
700 North Main Street
Fort Bragg, California
95437
(707) 964-9529

MC/V
Moderate

At the Pudding Creek Inn,
built in 1884 by a Russian
count, breakfast is served in
an enclosed flower-filled
fountain courtyard.

*Pudding Creek Inn
Fort Bragg, California*

MACLEAN HOUSE
P.O. Box 651
Inverness, California
94937
(415) 669–7392
Reservations:
(415) 663–1420

No credit cards
Moderate

This small, quiet, secluded guest house on Tomales Bay just north of San Francisco greets its guests with sherry and shortbread.

M A C L E A N   H O U S E

Scottish Shortbread

1 pound (4 sticks) softened
    unsalted butter
1 cup powdered sugar
3 cups sifted all-purpose
    flour

1 cup rice flour (or substitute
    1 additional cup all-
    purpose flour)

Preheat oven to 275°.

Cream butter and sugar. Blend well, but don't over-work. Gradually add flour. Turn dough on board lightly dusted with a mixture of powdered sugar and flour. Pat dough or roll gently into a 7" by 10" rectangle, $\frac{3}{8}$" thick. Place on baking sheet. Prick with fork. Mark with cutting lines. Refrigerate till cold. Cut apart and bake for about 40 minutes, until shortbread is sand-colored. Yields 20 pieces.

L A M O T H E   H O U S E

Lamothe House Pecan Pralines

1½ cups granulated sugar
½ cup brown sugar
½ stick (4 tablespoons)
    butter
½ cup evaporated milk

1 teaspoon vanilla
½ cup chopped or whole
    pecans
1 pinch baking soda

Butter cookie sheet or line with waxed paper.

Cook sugars and milk over medium heat, stirring until mixture starts to boil. Add butter, pecans and soda. Cook, stirring occasionally until it reaches the soft ball stage (when a bit of the candy dropped in cold water forms a soft ball) or 238° on a candy thermometer. Remove from fire and beat with spoon until mixture is creamy and begins to thicken. Drop by teaspoonfuls onto cookie sheet. (If mixture becomes too hard, return to heat and add a little water.) Makes 12 large or 24 small pralines.

LAMOTHE HOUSE
621 Esplanade Avenue
New Orleans, Louisiana
70116
(504) 947–1161

MC/V/AE
Very expensive

One of New Orleans's classic bed and breakfast inns, the Lamothe House captures all the charm of the city's French Quarter.

C L E F T S T O N E   M A N O R

Petticoat Tails

1½ cups (3 sticks) butter
1 cup granulated sugar
2 teaspoons vanilla
1½ tablespoons milk

3¾ cups unsifted all-purpose
   flour
3 tablespoons powdered
   sugar (optional)

Preheat oven to 325°.

With electric mixer, beat butter, sugar and vanilla until light and fluffy. Stir in milk and flour using a wooden spoon, then mix with hand until dough is smooth. Divide dough into 3 parts. On ungreased cookie sheets, roll out dough, one part at a time, into ¼" thick 9" rounds. Place 7" plate in centers of rounds, and cut around plate with a fluted pastry cutter. Remove plate. Cut into 8 sections. Bake 25 minutes. Cool completely. Sprinkle with confectioner's sugar if desired.

CLEFTSTONE MANOR
92 Eden Street
Bar Harbor, Maine
04609
(207) 288–4951

MC / V / AE
Moderate to expensive

Located on a windswept cliff at the foot of Cadillac Mountain, the century-old Cleftstone Manor offers a relaxing refuge from everyday life.

Cleftstone Manor
Bar Harbor, Maine

THE VICTORIAN VILLA
Hazelnut and Currant Scones

2 cups all-purpose flour
2 teaspoons baking powder
½ cup sugar
⅓ cup butter

2 eggs
¼ cup milk
½ cup chopped hazelnuts
½ cup Zante currants (dried)

Preheat oven to 375°. Line baking sheet with parchment paper.

Mix flour, baking powder and sugar. Rub butter into the flour mixture. Beat together eggs and milk, and stir into dry ingredients. Add hazelnuts and currants. Knead mixture 20 times, and roll out ½″ to ¾″ thick. Cut scones with a fluted round biscuit cutter. Bake for 12 to 18 minutes. Serves 8.

The Victorian Villa
Union City, Michigan

VICTORIAN VILLA

Victorian Villa Wassail

The Victorian Villa has a very special Christmas season which is celebrated Dickens-style, with wassail, plus puddings, trifles, hickory nut cakes and roasted chestnuts.

1 gallon fresh apple juice
1 quart fresh strained
  cranberry juice
1½ cups sugar
1 tablespoon aromatic bitters

4 cinnamon sticks
1 tablespoon whole allspice
2 oranges studded with
  cloves
2 cups dark rum

Combine ingredients and heat gently. Serve warm. Serves 20 to 25.

HARBIN HOT SPRINGS

Anna's Lemonade

2½ cups honey (star thistle
  or other light honey)
2½ cups water
2 cups fresh lemon juice, or
  to taste

water
3 tablespoons spearmint
  leaves

Blend honey, 2½ cups water and lemon juice in a blender. Put in a gallon container. Fill to ¾ of a gallon with additional water. Add spearmint leaves and allow to steep. Serve over ice. Yields 16 cups.

THE VICTORIAN VILLA
601 North Broadway
Union City, Michigan
49094
(517) 741-7383

MC / V
Moderate to expensive

The Victorian Villa is a 19th-century mansion run by innkeepers who are established experts on the custom of afternoon tea.

HARBIN HOT SPRINGS
P.O. Box 782
Middletown, California
95461
(707) 987-2477

No credit cards
Inexpensive to moderate

This 1,100-acre bathing-suit-optional hot springs resort is set in the hills just above northern California's Napa Valley.

INNSBRUCK INN
233 West Main Street
Aspen, Colorado
81611
(303) 925-2980

MC / V / AE / CB / DC
Expensive to very
expensive

At the family-operated
Innsbruck Inn, guests will
enjoy a breakfast buffet before a busy day on the
slopes, and a sauna and
glass of wine après ski.
Many friendships are
formed here, and groups
return together year after
year.

I N N S B R U C K   I N N

Champagne Punch

2 cups sugar   4½ cups orange juice
4 cups water   2 cups grapefruit juice
½ cup lemon juice   2 cups Rhine wine
½ cup lime juice   1 bottle champagne

In a saucepan, combine sugar with 2 cups water and lemon
juice and boil one minute. Add remaining water and let cool.
Stir in lime, orange and grapefruit juices. Pour into bowl filled
with ice. Add wine and champagne just before serving. Yields
approximately 30 servings.

G U S T A V U S   I N N

Spruce Tip Beer

green tips of spruce branches   boiling water
    (gathered in early   sugar
    spring)*   yeast

In early spring, gather a peck of new bright green tips of the
spruce branches. Cover with boiling water, and let the mixture cool. Drain the liquid from the spruce tips and to 2½ gal-
lons of the liquid add 2 pounds of sugar and ⅛ teaspoon of
yeast dissolved in 2 tablespoons of water. Stir all together until
sugar and yeast are completely dissolved. Bottle immediately
and store in a warm place for 4 or 5 days before opening. Chill
bottles before opening. Each gallon fills about ten 12-ounce
bottles. This is a cooling non-alcoholic drink.

*If spruce tips are gathered when no longer tiny and new,
the beer will take on a strong flavor and will be so effervrs-
cent that the bottles may burst.

G U S T A V U S   I N N
Raspberry Shrub

cider vinegar   sugar
raspberries   soda water or cold water

Pour enough cider vinegar over raspberries to cover the berries. Let this stand, covered with a clean cloth, for 24 hours to 2 days. Strain through a couple thicknesses of cheese-cloth, squeezing the berries to extract all the juice. To every pint of liquid, add a scant cup of sugar. Bring to a boil, and boil gently for 20 minutes. Let cool slightly, and pour into glass jars or bottles. Keep in a cool, dark place until needed. Serve as a beverage, pouring 2 tablespoons of the shrub over ice cubes and filling the glass to the top with cold water or soda water. Each cup of shrub makes 8 drinks.

GUSTAVUS INN
Box 60
Gustavus, Alaska
99826
(907) 697–2254

No credit cards
Expensive

This 7-room summertime Glacier Bay inn offers delightful local dishes, with fresh fish and eggs, vegetables picked from the garden, and berries for jam plucked from bushes in nearby fields and forests.

Gustavus Inn
Gustavus, Alaska

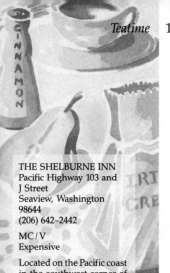

THE SHELBURNE INN
Pacific Highway 103 and
J Street
Seaview, Washington
98644
(206) 642–2442

MC / V
Expensive

Located on the Pacific coast
in the southwest corner of
Washington state, the Shelburne Inn has 14 rooms and
a restaurant that serves
nationally-acclaimed
cuisine.

CAPTAIN JEFFERDS INN
P.O. Box 691
Kennebunkport, Maine
04046
(207) 967–2311

No credit cards
Moderate to expensive

This mansion, a former sea
captain's residence, was
built in 1804. Captain
Jefferds' 11 rooms are filled
with antiques, art, and
flowers, and the inn allows
pets, if well-behaved.

S H E L B U R N E   I N N
Lemon Curd

Originally created as a tea-time condiment for scones and crumpets, lemon curd is also delicious on muffins, toast, waffles or pancakes.

*1 cup fresh-squeezed lemon
    juice*
*7 tablespoons lemon zest (the
    outermost part of lemon
    rind)*

*1 pound (about 2 cups)
    sugar*
¼ pound (1 stick) butter
8 eggs, lightly beaten

Combine lemon juice, zest, sugar and butter in double boiler over simmering water until sugar dissolves and butter melts. Whisk eggs into lemon mixture and keep stirring until thick (about 20 minutes). Remove from heat, cool and store in refrigerator. Yields about 5 cups.

C A P T A I N   J E F F E R D S   I N N
Holiday Hot Mulled Wine

3 whole allspice
6 whole cloves
5 cinnamon sticks
2 cups water
½ cup sugar

*2 lemons, seeded and thinly
    sliced*
*1 bottle claret (or comparable
    red wine)*

Enclose allspice, cloves and cinnamon sticks in cheesecloth and tie. Combine 2 cups water with sugar, add bag of spices and bring mixture to a boil. Lower heat and simmer for 10 minutes. Remove from burner. Add lemon slices, cover, and let the mixture stand for at least 20 minutes. Add claret and cook over medium heat until hot but not boiling for 10 minutes. Remove spice bag and serve. Serves 6.

B R I A R   R O S E   B   &   B

Strawberry Preserves

4 cups strawberries, cleaned   3 cups sugar
   and hulled

To make more or less preserves, use ¾ cup sugar for every cup of strawberries. Place strawberries in a bowl, layering with sugar. Allow to stand for 12 hours. In a saucepan, bring quickly to boiling point and simmer for 15 minutes. Place in a crock or enamel bowl, cover and allow to steep for another 12 hours. Return to pot just to reheat, then put the preserves in sterilized jars. Seal with paraffin. Yields 2 pints.

Orange Marmalade

2 large oranges   11 cups water
2 large lemons   8 cups sugar

Cut fruit into quarters and remove seeds. Soak the fruit in the water for 24 hours. Drain, reserving the liquid. Cut pulp into shreds. Return to the soaking water and boil for one hour. Add the sugar. Boil until juice forms a jelly. Cool, and put in hot sterilized jars. Seal with paraffin. (Add more lemons if a tarter marmalade is preferred. Emily Hunter at Briar Rose makes her marmalade on the tart side and uses coarsely cut rind.) Yields 2 quarts.

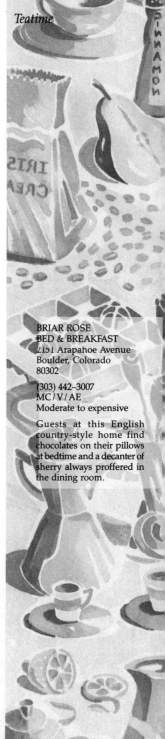

BRIAR ROSE
BED & BREAKFAST
2151 Arapahoe Avenue
Boulder, Colorado
80302

(303) 442–3007
MC / V / AE
Moderate to expensive

Guests at this English country-style home find chocolates on their pillows at bedtime and a decanter of sherry always proffered in the dining room.

THE WEDGWOOD INN
111 West Bridge Street
New Hope, Pennsylvania
18938
(215) 862–2570

No credit cards
Moderate to expensive

The innkeepers of this Victorian mansion in New Hope promise to make their guests' stays as pleasant as the surroundings.

THE WEDGWOOD INN
Hot Buttered Wedgwood

Carl Glassman makes his own liqueur, which he calls Wedgwood Almond Liqueur, to use in this recipe. A carafe of the liqueur is served to guests at their bedside as part of the evening ritual.

2 ounces almond liqueur
1 cup hot tea, cider or apple juice
1 tablespoon whipped unsalted butter

twist of orange peel
cinnamon stick

Pour almond liqueur in a mug. Fill with hot tea, cider or juice. Add butter and orange peel twist. Garnish with a cinnamon stick.

The Wedgwood Inn
New Hope, Pennsylvania

C I D E R   M I L L
Hot Spiced Cider

On frosty weekends in the fall and winter, Cider Mill keeps their hot spiced cider in an electric percolator, so it will be ready for all visitors. On extra cold nights servings are fortified with a shot of rum.

2 teaspoons whole cloves
2 teaspoons whole allspice
2 sticks cinnamon (3" each)

1 gallon apple cider
⅔ cup sugar
2 whole oranges, washed

Tie spices in cheesecloth or place in a tea ball. Pour cider in a large pot (a stock pot works well) and add spices, sugar, and oranges. Heat to boiling. Cover and simmer for 20 minutes.

D E E P   C R E E K   L O D G E
Crab Apple Liqueur

1 pound red crab apples
  (approximately) per
  quart jar

1 cup sugar per quart jar
2 cups vodka (approximately)
  per quart jar

Wash and remove stems from ripe red crab apples. Cut into quarters. Pack into quart jars up to an inch from the top. Add one cup sugar to each jar. Pour vodka over apples and sugar until it just reaches the surface. Seal the jars. Place sealed jars on their sides in a cool storage room. Turn once a day for 25 to 28 days. Then strain the liquid through a sieve and again through a fine strainer. When you are satisfied with its clarity, bottle in clean gin or vodka bottles. For a clearer drink, you may want to decant it after a few days. Do not throw away the pulp, but put it back into the jars, and carefully pour off the remaining liquid. Eventually when there is very little setting out, you can discard the pulp.

CIDER MILL
P.O. Box 441
Zoar, Ohio
44697
(216) 874–3133

MC / V
Moderate

A renovated mill built in 1863 houses this 2-room inn, located in the heart of northern Ohio's Amish country.

DEEP CREEK INN
P.O. Box 316
Maples, Idaho
83847
(208) 267–2373

MC / V
Inexpensive

This family-oriented 12-room country inn overlooks a creek in a setting that is appealing in any season. Guests can enjoy the landscape on the inn's bicycles.

BISHOPSGATE INN
Goodspeed Landing
East Haddam,
Connecticut
06423
(203) 873–1677

No credit cards
Moderate

Within walking distance of
the famous Goodspeed
Opera House, this 1818
colonial home is also near
many sites of historical in-
terest.

B I S H O P S G A T E   I N N
Minted Raspberry Cooler Bishopsgate Inn

½ cup fresh mint leaves
   plus mint sprigs for
   garnish
1 cup boiling water
one 6-ounce can frozen
   lemonade concentrate

1 pint fresh raspberries
   crushed and sweetened
   with ½ cup sugar (or
   one 10-ounce package
   frozen raspberries)
2 cups cold water

Combine ½ cup mint leaves and boiling water. Let steep 5 minutes. Add raspberries and frozen lemonade concentrate. Stir (until thawed, if frozen raspberries are used). Strain into pitcher half-filled with crushed ice. Add cold water and stir. Garnish with fresh mint leaves. Serves 8.

T H E   O K E M O   I N N
Bourbon Slush

2 cups boiling water
4 tea bags
2 cups sugar
7 cups cold water
2 cups bourbon

one 6-ounce can frozen
   lemonade concentrate
one 12-ounce can frozen
   orange juice concentrate
12 sprigs of mint

Combine the boiling water with the tea bags and allow to steep 4 to 5 minutes. Add the sugar, cold water, bourbon and 2 frozen juice concentrates in a large bowl or pot. Mix all together well, until frozen juice concentrates are fully thawed and blended. Pour into a large plastic bowl or other unbreakable container, and place in the freezer overnight.

To serve, spoon "slush" into four 6-ounce serving cups or glasses, and garnish each with a sprig of mint. Serve with a spoon. Serves 12. Keeps indefinitely in the freezer.

THE OKEMO INN
R.F.D. 1, Box 133
Ludlow, Vermont
05149
(802) 228–8834

All major credit cards
Moderate

Named after the mountain
that towers in the back-
ground, the 12-room Oke-
mo Inn offers summer golf
and winter ski packages.

Part 4

HORS D'OEUVRES

Hors d'Oeuvres

Many of the recipes in the preceding chapter on tea are also suitable for hors d'oeuvres. Indeed, many inns offer sherry or other wines right along with tea, forming a consolidated teatime–cocktail hour. Inns that follow the custom of wine and hors d'oeuvres usually do so between 6:00 and 8:00 P.M., when guests have had a chance to relax in their rooms and change into evening clothes, then congregate for a little conviviality before a night on the town.

Innkeepers at the Wedgwood in New Hope, Pennsylvania, serve a house liqueur in their blue-and-cream-colored parlor. While sipping a Wedgwood liqueur, one can sit in the bay window and chat with a friend or play Scrabble® or Trivial Pursuit®.

San Francisco's Petite Auberge offers hors d'oeuvres around the fireplace in the lower parlor. Guests gather to discuss their day in the city and make plans for dinner that evening.

The hors d'oeuvres dishes in this book will be interesting additions to your next party tray. With such selections as Tom's Treat, *Huîtres des Gourmets* and Goat Cheese Turnovers, you'll be able to introduce your guests to some exciting new treats.

SOCIETY HILL HOTEL

Arlene's Artichokes

cooking oil for deep frying
30 artichoke hearts,
    parboiled; or 3 cans of
    artichokes packed in
    water (approximately 10
    per can), drained
6 eggs, lightly beaten

2 cups Italian bread crumbs
1½ cups (3 sticks) butter
juice of 1½ lemons
3 cloves garlic, minced
3 teaspoons minced chives
Parmesan cheese to taste

Cut artichokes in half. Dip in beaten egg and coat with bread crumbs. Deep-fry until golden brown. Put on serving plate and keep warm. Melt butter, add lemon juice, garlic and chives.

Pour butter sauce over artichoke hearts and sprinkle with Parmesan cheese. Serves 6.

SOCIETY HILL HOTEL
OF PHILADELPHIA
301 Chestnut Street
Philadelphia,
Pennsylvania 19106
(215) 925-1919

MC / V / AE
Expensive

Located in Philadelphia's Historic Park, the Society Hill Hotel offers entertainment at its piano bar and fresh flowers and chocolates in each of its 12 rooms.

Society Hill Hotel
Philadelphia, Pennsylvania

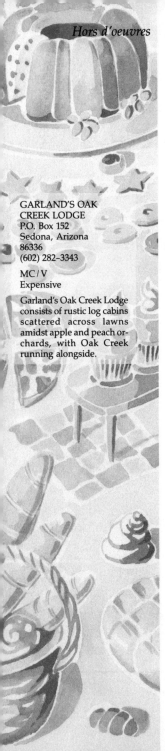

GARLAND'S OAK
CREEK LODGE
P.O. Box 152
Sedona, Arizona
86336
(602) 282-3343

MC / V
Expensive

Garland's Oak Creek Lodge
consists of rustic log cabins
scattered across lawns
amidst apple and peach orchards, with Oak Creek
running alongside.

GARLAND'S OAK CREEK LODGE

Wild Mushroom Paté

½ pound (2 sticks) unsalted
  butter
½ yellow onion, chopped
2 cloves garlic, minced
1½ pounds fresh boletus
  mushrooms, gently
  rinsed and chopped

1 tablespoon fresh parsley
1 tablespoon fresh thyme
½ cup dry white wine
⅛ cup dry sherry
salt and pepper to taste

Melt butter, add onion and garlic, and cook gently for a
minute. Add boletus, parsley and thyme, and cook over
moderate heat until mushrooms give off their juices. Stir in
wine and sherry. Cook, stirring occasionally, until liquid is
reduced and thickened slightly. Cool briefly, then purée in
food processor until smooth. Season to taste with salt and
pepper. Pour into individual ramekins and chill until set.
Serve with minced red onion and toast. Serves 4 to 6.

Garland's Oak Creek Lodge
Sedona, Arizona

T R O U T B E C K

Goat Cheese and Seafood Turnovers

DOUGH:

¼ cup heavy cream   2 cups all-purpose flour
¼ cup sour cream   salt and pepper to taste
1 egg

Combine heavy cream, sour cream and egg, then mix in flour, salt and pepper. Knead dough on floured surface until smooth. Let rest one hour in refrigerator, then roll out ⅛″ thick. Cut circles with a 2″ cookie cutter. While dough is chilling, prepare:

CHEESE FILLING:

½ pound chèvre   pinch of salt
¼ pound muenster   pinch of nutmeg
⅛ teaspoon pepper

Crumble cheese together. Mix in spices and set aside.

SEAFOOD STUFFING:

1 large onion, minced   ⅓ pound clams, chopped
1 small green pepper, diced   salt and pepper to taste
⅓ pound scallops, chopped   pinch each of oregano, cumin
⅓ pound shrimp, peeled, de-   and flour
   veined and chopped   2 tablespoons water

Sauté onion until transparent. Add pepper, seafood, seasonings and water. Cook for 2 minutes while stirring. Set aside and let cool.

ASSEMBLY:

Brush edges of dough circles with water. Place ½ teaspoon of filling in middle. Fold dough over filling, like a turnover. Using the tines of a fork, press along edge of turnover, sealing well. Heat oil for frying. Place turnovers in oil and fry on each side until golden brown. Yields approximately 6 dozen turnovers.

TROUTBECK
Leedsville Road
Amenia, New York
12501
(914) 373–9681

AE
Very expensive

This posh 422-acre country estate operates as an inn on the weekends and a conference center during the week and has been praised by *New York* Magazine, *The New York Times*, *Good Housekeeping* and *Country Living*.

C E N T E R   L O V E L L   I N N

Antipasti

ANCHOVY BUTTER:

1 cup (2 sticks) softened
   unsalted butter

3 tablespoons mashed
   anchovy fillets (rinsed
   free of salt)

Whip butter with electric mixer and beat in anchovy fillets. Can be used in sauces or, with pastry tube, to decorate canapes and vegetables. This recipe and the following serve 10 to 15.

MARINATED CARROTS:

1 pound tender young
   carrots
¾ cup dry white wine
¾ cup white wine vinegar
4 cups water
6 tablespoons oil
2 cloves garlic
small bunch parsley, minced

1 teaspoon sugar
1 teaspoon salt
pinch Cayenne pepper
1 teaspoon prepared Dijon
   mustard
1 teaspoon chopped fresh
   basil (or ½ teaspoon
   dry basil)

Wash and scrape carrots and cut into strips. Put wine, wine vinegar, water oil, garlic cloves, parsley, sugar, salt and Cayenne pepper into a small pot. Bring to a boil and simmer aproximately 10 minutes or until carrots are cooked *al dente*. Allow to cool in pot. Lift out carrots with slotted spoon and place on a serving dish. Boil liquid marinade down until about 2 cups remain. Mix in mustard and pour over carrots. Sprinkle with basil and chill.

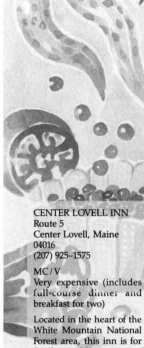

C E N T E R   L O V E L L   I N N

ONIONS IN VINEGAR:

24 small, even-sized white onions	*1 tablespoon dried tarragon (or one small bunch)*
6 small hot peppers	*6 cups boiling white wine vinegar*

Peel onions and place in a jar with bits of peppers and tarragon. Cover with boiling vinegar and marinate in a cool place for at least one week. Drain. Again, cover with fresh boiling vinegar, seal and store. Chill before use. Refrigerate jar when opened.

SWEET PEPPERS:

8 red sweet peppers	*½ teaspoon each, salt and pepper*
2 tablespoons red wine vinegar	*garlic clove, minced*
⅛ cup olive oil	

Roast peppers in the oven, or over the flame of a gas jet, until blackened. Peel off skin under running cold water. Seed, and cut into long strips. Marinate for at least one hour in vinegar, olive oil, salt, pepper and garlic.

CENTER LOVELL INN
Route 5
Center Lovell, Maine
04016
(207) 925-1575

MC / V
Very expensive (includes full-course dinner and breakfast for two)

Located in the heart of the White Mountain National Forest area, this inn is for families and features gourmet Italian cuisine.

*Center Lovell Inn
Center Lovell, Maine*

SCHNEIDER HAUS
Route 100, Box 2834
Duxbury, Vermont
05676
(802) 244–7726

MC / V / AE
Moderate

The 10-room Schneider
Haus was built entirely by
its innkeepers.

S C H N E I D E R   H A U S
Hot Mustard Sauce

½ cup dry mustard
½ cup white vinegar
1 egg

½ cup sugar
cream cheese and crackers

Mix together dry mustard and wine vinegar. Let stand overnight or longer. Beat in egg and sugar. Cook in the top of a double boiler over boiling water for 18 minutes over high heat, stirring to prevent coagulation. Serve over cream cheese with crackers. This quantity of sauce will cover 4 to 8 ounces cream cheese and will keep for a couple of months in the refrigerator.

T H E   H O M E S T E A D   I N N
Les Huîtres des Gourmets

duxelles (see following
recipe)

12 oysters on the half shell
3 tablespoons garlic butter

Place oysters on an oven-proof dish. Dab duxelles and garlic butter on each, and bake for 5 minutes. Serve garnished with lemon. Serves 4.

DUXELLES:

1 tablespoon butter
1 tablespoon minced onion
½ pound mushrooms,
* minced*

1 tablespoon minced
* shallots*
1 tablespoon heavy cream
salt and pepper to taste

Melt butter in sauté pan. Sauté onions until they begin to color. Add mushrooms and shallots and cook until liquids are rendered and then evaporate. Add a little cream and cook until reduced to a paste-like consistency. Season with salt and pepper to taste.

THE HOMESTEAD INN

Casserole d'Escargots

24 snails
5 ounces chanterelle
   mushrooms
1 tablespoon butter
2 teaspoons minced shallots

4 tablespoons garlic butter
½ cup heavy cream
½ teaspoon (a splash)
   Pernod (optional)

In a sauté pan, sauté snails and chanterelles in butter with shallots. Add garlic butter (see following recipe), let melt, and swirl around pan. Stir in heavy cream and Pernod and allow mixture to reduce somewhat. Sprinkle with chopped parsley and serve at once. Serves 4.

GARLIC BUTTER:

Mince large clove of garlic. Melt ¼ cup of softened butter in small pan. Add garlic, minced parsley, salt and pepper to taste.

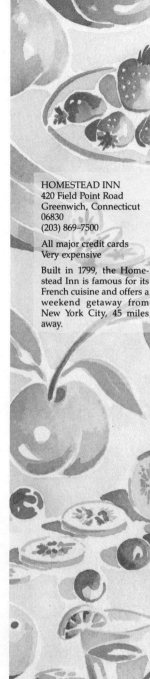

HOMESTEAD INN
420 Field Point Road
Greenwich, Connecticut
06830
(203) 869–7500

All major credit cards
Very expensive

Built in 1799, the Homestead Inn is famous for its French cuisine and offers a weekend getaway from New York City, 45 miles away.

Homestead Inn
Greenwich, Connecticut

T H E   B R A M B L E   I N N

Caponata

*2 pounds eggplant, peeled
  and cubed (½" cubes)*
salt
½ cup olive oil
2 cups finely-chopped celery
*¾ cup finely-chopped
  onions*
*⅓ cup wine vinegar mixed
  with 4 teaspoons sugar*

*3 cups drained whole-pack
  tomatoes*
2 tablespoons tomato paste
*6 large green olives, pitted
  and slivered*
2 tablespoons capers
*4 anchovy fillets, rinsed,
  pounded flat and smooth*
freshly ground pepper

Sprinkle eggplant cubes generously with salt and set them in a colander to drain. After 35 minutes, pat cubes dry with paper towels and set aside. Heat ¼ cup olive oil in a heavy skillet. Add celery and cook for 10 minutes over moderate heat, stirring often. Stir in onions and cook for an additional 8 to 10 minutes, or until onions and celery are soft and lightly colored. With a slotted spoon transfer them to a bowl. Add remaining ¼ cup oil to skillet and sauté eggplant until it is lightly browned, stirring constantly. Return celery and onions to skillet. Add remaining ingredients. Bring to a boil and simmer uncovered for 15 minutes, stirring often. Flavor to taste with additional salt, pepper and vinegar. Refrigerate until ready to serve. Makes 8 cups, enough for 20 servings.

THE BRAMBLE INN

Best Liver Paté

¾ cup chopped scallions
1 clove garlic, minced
½ pound (2 sticks) butter
1 pound chicken livers
3 tablespoons cognac

⅛ teaspoon thyme
1½ teaspoons dry mustard
a dash each of nutmeg,
    cloves, mace
salt and pepper to taste

Sauté scallions and garlic in 3 tablespoons butter. Remove
from pan. In same pan, sauté livers a few at a time in 2 tablespoons butter. Remove from sauté pan while slightly pink
inside. Add cognac to pan. Ignite and pour over livers in an
oven-proof dish. Put livers through fine-blade food grinder.
Blend in the rest of the butter and spices. Add scallions and
garlic and mix well. Season with salt and pepper to taste. Pour
into mold. Chill until firm. To serve, unmold on platter or
serve individual slices on bed of lettuce. Serves 12 to 15.

THE INN AT PERRY CABIN

Oysters Perry Cabin

40 fresh-shucked oysters on
    the half-shell
10 slices bacon, quartered

1½ cups grated cheddar
    cheese

Leave oysters on the deep side of the shell, discarding other
half of shell. Top each oyster with a bit of cheese and a piece
of bacon. Broil for 5 minutes, or until bacon is crisp. Serve
immediately (you can serve on a bed of rock salt to help re-
tain heat). Serves 6 to 8.

THE BRAMBLE INN
P.O. Box 807
Brewster, Massachusetts
02631
(508) 896-7644

MC/V/AE for meals only
Moderate

This Cape Cod inn is a
haven for sports lovers,
with the beach a 5-minute
walk away, tennis courts ad-
jacent, and golf and fishing
nearby.

THE INN AT
PERRY CABIN
308 Watkins Lane
St. Michaels, Maryland
21663
(301) 745-5178

MC/V/AE
Very expensive

Situated on the serene
Miles River in the historic
village of St. Michaels, this
6-room inn offers guests
nearby sailing, antiquing
and spectacular water fowl
watching.

OLD RITTENHOUSE
INN
301 Rittenhouse Avenue
Bayfield, Wisconsin
54814
(715) 779-5111

Moderate

This is an historic 30-room
mansion filled with an-
tiques and 12 working fireplaces. Put your feet up and
relax on the porch overlooking Lake Superior.

O L D   R I T T E N H O U S E   I N N

Picante Cheesecake

1 pound Roquefort cheese
4 cups sour cream
2 cups grated Parmesan
   cheese

3 pounds cream cheese
2 cups picante sauce
16 eggs

Preheat oven to 350°. Prepare springform cheesecake pans by brushing with melted butter and lining with bread crumbs. This makes 4 cheesecakes, 11″ across.

Mix all ingredients. Pour into pans. Top with more bread crumbs. Bake at 350° for one hour and 15 minutes. Bake cheesecakes sitting in or on trays of water. Cool in oven for one hour with oven door ajar.

V I C T O R I A N   F A R M H O U S E

Toasted Clam Rolls

three 6½-ounce cans minced
   clams
⅓ cup thinly-sliced green
   onion
½ cup mayonnaise
6 tablespoons grated
   Parmesan cheese

1 teaspoon Worcestershire
   Sauce
¾ teaspoon garlic powder
½ teaspoon liquid hot pepper
   seasoning
1 large 24-ounce loaf thin-
   sliced sandwich bread
6 tablespoons melted butter

Preheat oven to 425°. Butter a baking sheet.

Drain clams well, reserving liquid for other cooking uses. Combine clams, green onions, mayonnaise, Parmesan cheese, Worcestershire Sauce, garlic powder and hot pepper seasoning.

VICTORIAN FARMHOUSE

Trim crusts from bread slices. With a rolling pin, flatten each slice until very thin. Spread about one tablespoon of clam mixture on each piece of bread, then roll up jellyroll fashion. Brush well with melted butter. Leave whole (for sandwiches) or cut in half (for appetizers). Arrange rolls 1" apart on baking sheet. Bake for 12 minutes, or until lightly browned. Makes 2 dozen finger sandwiches or 4 dozen appetizers.

BARNARD-GOOD HOUSE

Tom's Treat

4 juice oranges, squeezed
four 5½-ounce cans apricot
    nectar
2 fresh limes, squeezed
½ cup juice drained from
    crushed pineapple

6 tablespoons canned cream
    of coconut
1 cup vodka or rum
    (optional)

Mix all juices and shake well. Great for breakfast. For an evening drink, add crushed ice and vodka or rum. Serves 8.

The Barnard-Good House
Cape May, New Jersey

VICTORIAN FARMOUSE
P.O. Box 357
Little River, California
95456
(707) 937–0697

No credit cards
Expensive

This countryside inn is set among orchards and flower gardens.

BARNARD-GOOD
HOUSE
238 Perry Street
Cape May, New Jersey
08204
(609) 884–5381

MC/V
Expensive

Good breakfasts and warmth are the hallmarks of this resort-town inn, which also promises luxurious bathing in a copper tub.

BRADFORD INN
Main Street
Bradford, New
Hampshire
03221
(603) 938–5309

No credit cards
Moderate

Owners of the Bradford Inn
claim that there's "simply
nothing to do" but relax, yet
in the same breath offer 3
ski areas, lakes Sunapee
and Massasecum, bicycles
and rooms filled with in-
teresting books.

LOCUST LAKE FARM
B & B
5590 Kessler Cowlesville
Road
West Milton, Ohio
45383
(513) 698–4743

Inexpensive

The hospitality is wonderful. Gourmet breakfast is
served in the dining room
or the cheerfully screened
porch. The Inn is tastefully
decorated and very com-
fortable.

THE BRADFORD INN

Liver Paté

1 stalk celery
3 sprigs parsley
6 whole peppercorns
1 quart water
1 pound chicken livers
½ medium onion
1 teaspoon salt

2 teaspoons dry mustard
½ teaspoon nutmeg
¼ teaspoon cloves
1 teaspoon Tabasco
½ clove garlic
1 cup (2 sticks) softened
    butter

Place celery, parsley and peppercorns in water and bring to
a boil. Add livers and simmer for 15 minutes. Drain. Put livers
and onions through food grinder, using finest blade. Blend
in remaining ingredients. Pack in a mold. Wrap, seal, date
and freeze. When ready to use, thaw in refrigerator. Makes
3 cups, serving 6 to 8.

LOCUST FARM B & B

Dried Fruit Cream Scones

2 cups all-purpose flour
1 tablespoon baking powder
½ teaspoon salt
¼ cup sugar

¾ cup chopped dried fruit
    (apricots, prunes,
    peaches)
½ cup golden raisins
1¼ cup heavy cream

GLAZE:
3 tablespoons butter, melted

2 tablespoons sugar

Preheat oven to 350°. Use an ungreased baking sheet.

Combine the first four ingredients, stirring with a fork to mix
well. Add dried fruit and raisins. Still using a fork, stir in
cream and mix until the dough holds together. Lightly flour
board and transfer dough to it. Knead dough 8 or 9 times.
Pat into a circle about 10" round.

For glaze, spread the butter over top of dough and sprinkle
with sugar on top. Cut the circle into 12 wedges and place
on baking sheet, allowing about 1" between pieces.

Bake for about 15 minutes, or until golden brown. Serves 12.

THE VERMONT INN
Bloody Mary

2 cups V-8 Juice
2 ounces lemon and lime
    juice, mixed
2 teaspoons horseradish
4 dashes of Tabasco Sauce
4 dashes of Worcestershire
    Sauce

¼ teaspoon celery salt
¼ teaspoon salt
¼ teaspoon pepper
6 ounces vodka
4 wedges lime
4 stalks celery

Mix V-8 Juice with lemon-lime mix, horseradish, Tabasco and Worcestershire sauces, salt, pepper and vodka. Shake with cracked ice and strain into 4 large glasses over ice cubes. Garnish each with a wedge of lime and stalk of celery. Serves 4.

THE VERMONT INN
Route 4
Killington, Vermont
05751
(802) 775-0708

MC/V/AE
Expensive

The Vermont Inn is a favorite for winter vacations, with the Killington and Pico ski areas just minutes away. Rates are lower in summer, when the tennis courts and swimming pool are enticing attractions.

HOTEL LENADO
Hotel Lenado Hot Artichoke Dip

two 14-ounce cans artichoke
    hearts (not the marinat-
    ed kind), drained and
    chopped
1 cup Parmesan cheese

1 cup shredded mozzarella
    cheese
1 cup mayonnaise
1 teaspoon salt
1 minced garlic clove

Preheat oven to 350°. Butter a soufflé dish or serving terrine.

Mix all ingredients thoroughly in a large bowl. Spoon mixture into prepared dish. Bake for 25 to 30 minutes. Serve hot with melba toast rounds or stoneground wheat crackers. Serves 10.

HOTEL LENADO
425 Rio Grande Place
Aspen, Colorado
81611
(303) 925-6246
Reservations:
(303) 925-9000

MC/V/AE
Very expensive

This upscale inn—a new Aspen landmark—offers hot tub, sauna, swimming pool, bicycles, and tennis court.

Index